BOUNCE THE BALLS & THEY WILL COME

A Coach's Passion for
the Great Commission

Betty Wiseman

Hall of Fame Coach

NEW HOPE
PUBLISHERS

BIRMINGHAM, AL

New Hope® Publishers
P. O. Box 12065
Birmingham, AL 35202-2065
www.newhopepublishers.com

New Hope Publishers is a division of WMU ®.

Library of Congress Cataloging-in-Publication Data
Wiseman, Betty, 1943-

  Bounce the balls and they will come : a coach's passion for the
Great Commission / Betty Wiseman.
       p. cm.

  ISBN 978-1-59669-245-9 (sc)
  1. Short-term missions. 2. Wiseman, Betty, 1943- 3. Sports--
Religious aspects--Christianity. I. Title.

  BV2082.S56W57 2011
  266'.023--dc22

                         2010043137

Cover design: Left Coast Design
Interior design: Michel Lê

ISBN-10: 1-59669-245-6
ISBN-13: 978-1-59669-245-9
N094140 • 0311 • 3M1

DEDICATION

To Linda Sue Wiseman McCown

JANUARY 12, 1939 ~ FEBRUARY 27, 2009

THIS BOOK IS DEDICATED TO THE MEMORY OF MY SISTER,
Linda McCown, who died suddenly but peacefully
on February 27, 2009, just four months prior to
the final draft of the manuscript for this book.
She was so excited that it would be published.

Linda was a constant source of inspiration and encouragement
to me by her positive outlook on life and deep faith in God.
In spite of her struggle through the years to battle diabetes,
an amputation that eventually put her in a wheelchair,
the loss of her beloved husband "Shag,"
and finally a dependence on dialysis to survive,
she continued to live each day to the fullest with
a smile on her face and joy in her heart.

Linda demonstrated to everyone who knew her how to live
joyfully under very difficult circumstances and reminded me
so often that God doesn't give us more than we are capable of
handling. She had her own ministry of encouragement to many
people from the confinement of her wheelchair.
Linda was my dear sister, but more than that, she was my friend.
I continue to miss her presence in my life,
but celebrate her eternal presence with our heavenly Father.

And, I look forward to a happy reunion when God calls me home.

CONTENTS

Wow Moments!
~ Gonzalo and Yinna
~ Opening New Doors
~ Outside the Fence
~ You Are the Church

CHAPTER 3
COMPASSION

Lay Your Trophies Down
Humbled
Love
Kindness
Spontaneity
Sensitivity
Caring
Patience
Listening
Willing to Give and Receive

CHAPTER 4
ENDURANCE

"I Am Serving My Jesus"
The Value of Hard Work
Overcoming Challenges
Hungry, If Only for the Night
Surprise! The Heat Is for Real!
All Kinds of Energy
Required Focus

CHAPTER 5
PREPARATION

Elvira
Preparing in the Wilderness
Sufficiency

PREFACE

Over the past several months, I have sensed that God is leading me to bring closure to my sports evangelism journey at Belmont University. It has been a difficult decision, but I know "[t]here is a time for everything, and a season for every activity under heaven" (Ecclesiastes 3:1). I have always prayed, *"Lord, give me wisdom to know what time it is in my life!"* What I mean is I want God to lead me in knowing the various seasons of my life, when to begin something and when to end something. It has been a wonderful season of sports evangelism for me over the past decade and a half. Of course, I will continue to be involved in fulfilling the Great Commission by going on missions trips through my church, and I will continue my administrative work with students here at Belmont.

God affirmed my decision on my most recent sports evangelism trip to Malta in May 2010. The island of Malta sits in the beautiful, blue Mediterranean Sea, about 100 miles off the coast of Sicily and a little more than 200 miles off the coast of Africa. The Apostle Paul, a prisoner on his way to Rome to be tried, was shipwrecked on the island of Malta for three months. "Once safely on shore, we found out that the island was called Malta" (Acts 28:1). The fact that God had called me to walk where Paul walked was significant to me, and served as a good way to end my Belmont sports evangelism ministry.

We stayed in a hotel on St. Paul's Bay where we walked down to the water's edge and looked out into the Mediterranean at a monument erected to honor Paul. We then visited Paul's Grotto, an underground cave, where Paul was imprisoned. Realizing that some of our Scripture may have been written from within these hewed out rock walls was overwhelming. That moment was a worship experience for me. We also walked inside a church that stands over the prison cave. Here Paul baptized the first converts to Christianity in Malta. I found our ministry there and the place itself to be a perfect closure to my season!

FOREWORD

One of them, an expert in the law,
tested him with this question:
"Teacher, which is the greatest commandment in the Law?"
Jesus replied, "'Love the Lord your God with all your heart
and with all your soul and with all your mind.'
This is the first and greatest commandment.
And the second is like it: 'Love your neighbor as yourself.'"

~ MATTHEW 22:35-39

W hen my husband, Dennis, and I were first married, we lived in a tiny apartment with one table, two chairs, a sofa, and a television that got three channels. We had one frying pan and 18 casserole dishes (wedding presents). We ate pork chops and green peas almost every night, because that was what I could cook.

I was in heaven. I loved that man so much, I didn't care where I was as long as I was with him.

This is how God intends us to love Him. "I will give them a heart to know me," He told Jeremiah. "They will return to me with all their hearts" (Jeremiah 24:7).

At revival services we used to sing, "Set My Soul Afire, Lord." I don't think we really meant it. I'm not even sure we understood what we were asking—to have our ambitions and agendas burned away, consumed by a passion for God and the people He so loves. Everything else pales in comparison. You love Him so much, you don't care where it leads, as long as you're with Him.

That's the kind of passion that marks Betty Wiseman's life.

I came to know Betty not long after the missions trip to Chile in 1992 that set her soul afire—the trip when, as she describes it, God "unzipped" her heart and showed her what her life was really going to be about.

Mind you, she had not been sitting on her hands up until that point. By the 1990s, Betty Wiseman was a champion athlete and coach, a pioneer in women's collegiate athletics. For a country girl from Portland, Tennessee, Betty had already written a large story with her life.

But God was writing Betty into an even larger story—His.

Betty described that process to me:

> There was a time when I thought Belmont University couldn't do without me; as a basketball coach I was so intense. My passions were caught up in where I was and my work. That doesn't mean that God wasn't important in my life, and I think through the years I've been able to be a witness, but I'd never been consumed with God. And [now] it's like, "Whoa! Why couldn't I have discovered this [total freedom in Christ] a long time ago?

The story Betty is living now blows her away. It captivates the people she coaches and those she embraces as she bounces balls around the world. I've traveled on missions trips with Betty, watched her work the sidelines of the Belmont University basketball court, and been the beneficiary of her influence in my own son's life. I've stood beside her in the choir loft almost every Sunday for 20 years. She sings like she coaches—with her whole heart. She is constantly wowed by God.

Betty Wiseman would never have been persuaded to write a story about herself. So you should know this is a story about God— about what He does with people who give Him their whole hearts. It's a story about what He might do with you.

~ KARLA WORLEY, AUTHOR OF *GROWING WEARY DOING GOOD?*

ACKNOWLEDGMENTS

NEW HOPE PUBLISHERS

BELMONT UNIVERSITY

FAMILY AND FRIENDS

THE LATE HERBERT C. GABHART ~ HELEN GABHART MISSIONS FUND

DR. NORMA BAKER GABHART ~ READER

TENNESSEE BAPTIST CONVENTION PARTNERSHIP
MISSIONS DEPARTMENT

KARLA WORLEY ~ FRIEND, AUTHOR, WORSHIP LEADER

PAUL AND DEBBIE CHENOWETH AND CHENOWETH DESIGNS

STUDENT-ATHLETES AND MEMBERS OF MISSIONS TEAMS

FAITHFUL DONORS

BRENTWOOD BAPTIST CHURCH (MY HOME CHURCH)

CREELY AND THE LATE BILL WILSON ~ FRIENDS IN MISSIONS

PRAYER PARTNERS

AGAPE II SUNDAY SCHOOL CLASS

MISSIONARIES ~ PASTORS ~ CHURCHES ~ VOLUNTEERS ~ TRANSLATORS

PHYLLIS COBB ~ WILCOX WORLD TRAVEL AND TOURS

INTRODUCTION

MY JOURNEY

THE CALL ~ JOHN 3:16

I stepped outside the quaint little church, taking a break from the meeting going on inside. I leaned on the partially collapsed wooden gate and surveyed the place. I needed to absorb the beauty, to capture a forever-picture in my mind and soul. The ever-present Andes Mountains in the distance provided a backdrop for two breathtaking snow-capped volcanoes, rolling hills, and the beautiful countryside. The setting was rustic, yet majestic and peaceful. The quietness and serenity soothed my soul and filled my spirit. I realized for the first time that this was just a speck in God's great universe, and I felt a deep desire to see and experience more. I was overwhelmed by God's presence and the beauty of this small, yet very important, piece of His world. I stood in awe, and I worshipped Him.

God, what am I doing here, so far away from home, in Temuco, in Chile, in South America? Why have You brought me here? Why does it feel so right to be here? I have never experienced You quite like this before. I praise You, and I worship You.

That experience, nearly 20 years ago, changed the course of my life's journey and gave me a new focus and passion. At that moment, God, Creator of the universe, became more real to me. He became a much bigger and more personal God. I began to see the world through His eyes and not my own. It was as if John 3:16 were written in the sky: "For God so loved the world that he gave his one and only Son, that whoever believes in Him shall not perish but have eternal life."

I believed God was saying to me, *This, Betty, is why you are here.*

A NEW WORLD OPENS UP

I had been aware of the tug on my heart to go on a missions trip for several years, but I just would not respond to the urging. I thought Belmont University, where I had been teaching for 26 years, could not do without me. As a coach and teacher, I was an intense and driven individual. My passions at that point in my life were caught up in where I was, what I could accomplish, and how I could be successful in my work. That doesn't mean that God wasn't important in my life, but I had never really allowed Him to have complete control.

In 1992, I went on a ten-day missions trip to Temuco, Chile. I was part of a seven-member Woman's Missionary Union volunteer team from Tennessee. We worked with career missionary Clara Brincefield (now Brincefield Huff) in local and rural churches throughout south Chile, conducting prayer retreats and missions activities. I sang, gave my testimony, witnessed, loved, hugged, and reached out to the people. I remembered a few words of Spanish from my college classes, but I communicated best with smiles, hugs, tears, and spirit—the language of the heart.

We visited several schools where we played games and talked with the children. Their little faces captured my heart. Everywhere we went I saw that the children had no playgrounds, no equipment to play with, and no gymnasiums. Their world for play was concrete, dirt, and a little grass—not very inviting.

Some people would consider the areas we visited Third World; there was no indoor plumbing and no electricity. Homes were mere shacks, and most were about the size of living rooms in Tennessee. I felt like I had gone back in time, to my childhood days growing up on a farm in rural Tennessee in the 1940s. This was my first foreign missions trip, and I knew it would not be my last.

When I returned to the US from Chile, I was in total shock, culture shock. The noise, the cars, the fast-paced racing from place to place, food, money, and things—where are we all going, and what are we doing? I felt depressed, sad, angry, frustrated, restless, and empty.

I had too many clothes in my closet, too much furniture in my condo, my car looked expensive, and I didn't need food. I wasn't even hungry. My needs changed, along with my priorities. I was different. A whole new world had opened up to me. God unzipped my heart, opened my eyes, and said, *OK, Betty, this is what it's all about; this is what I have been preparing you for.* Following my trip to Chile, my whole perspective changed. Whenever I walked out my front door, I saw the world differently. I didn't see just my community, my city, or my state. I saw a world, God's world. And I had been called into it. I found ways to incorporate my experiences into life lessons, and I shared them as often as possible, even in the classes I taught. My work at Belmont became more ministry-oriented, as I began to teach from a broader, world perspective.

I focused on questions such as how could I pass on what I had learned to my students, young adults with so much potential and their whole lives ahead of them? How could I use sports as a tool to reach people and share Christ? Could I get our student athletes involved in ministry? I wanted them to experience what I had experienced.

I also longed for the country and the people I had just encountered there. I cried, not knowing exactly why. Memories of the Chilean people tugged at my heart. I wanted more; more of the country, the language, the people, and the ministry. I felt very uncomfortable at home. I was searching and wrestling with God.

"Dear God," I prayed, *"What has happened to me? Why do I feel this way? My heart hurts, aches, for what I experienced. What does all this mean? Are you calling me back?"*

I waited for some relief from that uncomfortable feeling that God had placed on my heart, but it did not come. Knowing that I would begin a sabbatical leave from Belmont in the fall, my first extended break from teaching, I made a call to Clara. "What if I come back to Chile? What can I do? Where would I stay?"

Clara said, "Just pack your bags and come on. You can stay with me, and you will do what you have been doing at Belmont all these years. God will use your teaching, coaching, and love for people to minister here. Just come and trust Him. He will lead."

That was all the affirmation I needed to return. I started packing duffle bags with physical education activity equipment: playground balls, basketballs, wands, ropes, beanbags, a parachute, and anything else I could use with children for play and activity.

All the while, my mind filled with questions! Was I ready for something like this? Was I ready to receive what God had in store for me? Would I mess up? Could I trust God in all this? Did I really believe that He could use me? I questioned my readiness. But, I trusted that God would not be taking me back unless I was ready. "I have much more to say to you, more than you can now bear" (John 16:12).

> Just come and trust Him. He will lead.

I remember telling some friends who were visiting me during the summer when I first went to Chile (and this was prophetic): "I don't know what it is, but I feel like I'm about to begin a whole new phase of my life." They have reminded me of that statement many times. I guess I was just ready. God had prepared me for this moment in time. It was a step of faith for me, that first missions trip, and I was returning for more.

MY JOURNEY

Before I continue sharing more about what God has taught me through international sports evangelism, I want to say that the journey to where I am now did not begin with my first overseas missions trip in 1992. It all began back on a farm in rural Portland, Tennessee, where I grew up in a Christian family filled with love for one another and for God. It began in the First Baptist Church of Portland where I grew up literally "cutting my teeth" on God's Word and developing a love for missions...and teaching...and basketball.

A basketball goal, a rim without a net, attached to the wall of the barn loft was my first "court." There I created my own personal space for honing my shooting skills as a young basketball player. My very first years of competition came in junior high school where the gymnasiums and courts were small, with only the two goals and no seating space. However, high school afforded me opportunities to play in various gyms of all sizes throughout the mid-state. Over the years and in my travels around the world, I have learned a gym is a gym, and each one is unique because of the people it serves.

Betty Wiseman was inducted into the Tennessee Sports Hall of Fame in 2004.

I have lived my life in and around gymnasiums, enjoying a full career of playing, teaching, and coaching the game of basketball. The gym is my natural habitat, and sports is my passion. The sights, sounds, smells, and atmosphere of a basketball court make up my comfort zone. The bouncing of balls is rhythm to my ears.

Since my graduation from Belmont University in 1966, I have spent more than four decades serving in several capacities at the school. I was professor of health and physical education for 42 years, basketball coach for 16 years, associate dean of students for 3 years, and have been assistant athletic director for student services and senior woman administrator for the last 12 years. In 1968, I became a women's sports trailblazer when I founded the women's basketball program at Belmont, one of the first programs, not only in the state, but also in the southeast. I continued coaching and directing that successful basketball program, along with teaching full time, for more than a decade. Because of that pioneering work in women's sports, I have been honored by several organizations for contributions to collegiate athletics. In 1999, during the NCAA Women's Final Four in San Jose, California, I received the Josten-Berenson Service Award from the Women's Basketball Coaches Association in recognition of a lifelong commitment to women's basketball. And I was inducted into the Tennessee Sports Hall of Fame in 2004 for contributions to promoting women's basketball in the state. In July 2007, I was featured in a front-page article of *The Tennessean*, Nashville's local newspaper, as a Tennessee Sports Legend.

Teacher, coach, pioneer, "legend"—regardless of the role or accolades or titles, it has all come to me by the grace of God and His divine call on my life to service and ministry. You will see in this book how God used my "growing up" days and my time with my family and my work with college students to give me the true call on my life: sports evangelism. This is the story of my journey to a ministry in sports; the story of how God has orchestrated the course of my life, connected all the dots, and led me to this point and place in time. I am a product of a loving family, generous benefactors in the faith, a successful career using God-given talents in the arena of sports and teaching, and His faithfulness through the years. A call from God to be involved in missions, specifically to sports evangelism, has taken me all over the world and into gymnasiums and courts of all kinds: indoor, open-air, outdoor; concrete, grass, asphalt, dirt; rain-soaked, dark, dirty; small, medium and seldom large. Most of the time they had rims with no nets, no more than make-shift play areas. These experiences have led me to see the world through God's eyes and sports as an awesome platform for sharing the good news of Jesus Christ.

The stories and personal experiences within this book span nearly two decades of sports evangelism trips to countries throughout Central and South America, Europe, and Africa. These trips have transformed the lives of participants, sown seeds of God's love among thousands, and brought countless numbers of people into a personal relationship with Jesus Christ. They demonstrate principles of evangelism that you can use in lifestyle evangelism right now wherever you live. Throughout these pages, you will find yourself transported to countries and places of ministry that I hope will become real and personal to you, just as they are to me. I have included a few pictures that capture some of these special moments and places. There is also an appendix with some practical ideas that can be used in sports evangelism ministry.

This book is about my journey in faith, how I discovered my platform for telling the good news of Jesus Christ and developed a passion for leading others to do the same. It is also about the college athletes who accompany me on these sports evangelism trips. They are willing to say "yes, we will go" in spite of feelings of inadequacy. My desire is that God will use this book to inspire, encourage, motivate, and move you to action, causing you to discover and use whatever platform, or means, He has given you.

Miss Betty rejoices with
the littlest teammate, Josey Scott.

CHAPTER 1

BETTY, GO AND TELL!

EVANGELISM~ WHY?

S ometimes Scripture can become too familiar to Christians. Verses we quote from memory become just that. I learned the Great Commission, Matthew 28:19–20, as a child growing up in a Baptist church in missions organizations.

"Therefore go and make disciples of all nations, baptizing them in the name of the Father and of the Son and of the Holy Spirit, teaching them to obey everything I have commanded you. And surely I am with you always, to the very end of the age."

How many times had I quoted that Scripture in my lifetime? Many, but the Great Commission truly became real and urgent in my life during my initial missions trips to Chile, Scotland, and Poland in the 1990s. The message became personal: "Betty, go and tell!" I discovered that missions must become who we are and not what we do. And, this commission must become a part of our daily lives where we live and work. I had finally become a "guardian" of the Great Commission. I had begun to become obedient to our Lord's great command.

My place of work at Belmont University became my daily missions field. I became more sensitive to opportunities to share my faith in the classroom, in my office, and in interpersonal relationships. I prayed daily for an opportunity to share Christ. My office became a "prayer room" as more and more students discovered: "This teacher will pray with you." My spiritual life became entwined with my professional life. I couldn't tell where one began or the other ended. Real ministry had begun in my life. The world was outside my front door and stretched as far south as Chile, as far north as Scotland, and as far to the east as Poland. I was eager for the next call to leave my daily missions field to "go and tell" somewhere else, too.

Years of feeling inadequate vanished as I surrendered to God all my fears of witnessing and sharing my faith. I claimed Matthew 10:19–20: *"Do not worry about what to say or how to say it. At that time you will be given what to say, for it will not be you speaking, but the Spirit of your Father speaking through you."*

Oh, I still get butterflies each time I prepare to leave on a missions trip, just like I used to get when I prepared for each game. My confidence in the gym all those years was placed in my preparation and readiness. My confidence in sharing the gospel is in Christ, who sends me forth in His name.

I often think about a story I read long ago in a missions magazine. Missionaries went into a remote part of Africa and shared the Jesus film with a tribe. Following the film, the missionaries gave an invitation to follow Christ, and the entire tribe came forward to pray to receive Christ.

The following night the missionaries showed the film once more, not sure the tribe really understood what they did. Only a few minutes into the film the tribe's chief stepped forward and asked the missionaries to stop the film. He said:

"You do not need to show us this again. You see, we have known there is a God, but we just didn't know how to get to Him. Last night we learned the way is through His Son, Jesus. We have been waiting for someone to tell us the way."

This story haunts me! There are people all over the world waiting for someone to show them the way. I feel an urgent call to go and tell others that the way to God is through Jesus Christ. I must go and tell!

BOUNCING BALLS AND TALL AMERICANS = A GREAT PLATFORM

It was Friday morning in Rio de Janeiro, Brazil, and we were scheduled to go to another part of the city, Costa Barros, to work with a local pastor planning a church start. We were to hold basketball clinics in the local favela (slum) and work with the children to draw attention to the church starters. We climbed a quarter-mile hill with our bags of basketballs to discover a small concrete court enclosed by a fence, sitting in the blazing-hot sun. It was surrounded by small homes (shacks), stacked on top of one another, but there was no one in sight. We looked around and wondered what we were going to do.

"Get the basketballs out and start playing. Bounce he Balls and they will come," I said.

Tall American athletes dribbling basketballs through the streets are all it takes to draw a crowd. I had seen this scenario many times on other missions trips. One by one, two by two, they came. The pastor and I took two of our players and two balls, and for 30 minutes we walked the streets of that slum, dribbling the balls and inviting the children and adults to come. When we finally climbed the hill once again, there were several hundred children, barefoot or in flip-flops, running and playing with our team. Adults, young and old, stood outside the fence to watch.

For years now this has been my platform as I go with athletes from Belmont and share Christ internationally, "Bounce the balls and they will come." Whether we are drumming up attendance or on a scheduled visit to a local school, the routine is always the same. It doesn't matter if we have 30 minutes or two hours. We have the children sit around the court and give a brief demonstration of full-court basketball. When they see the skill level of the college athletes and know that they are legitimate players, we have the audience's attention and trust.

After our brief demonstration game, we invite the children to join us on the court for fun relays involving dribbling, passing, and shooting skills. They become competitive, and that is when the fun begins. We might then have them play against or with us in a mock game. They all want to play the Americans.

Depending on the amount of time we have, we adjust our routine to end with a time of sharing greetings, testimonies, and the gospel. Just imagine 600 children playing and having fun then sitting in complete silence as they listen to what we have to say. It is only through the power of the Holy Spirit that this can happen. We view each session as a divine appointment orchestrated by God.

And we're not ministering only to the children. I am always drawn to the adults who are watching the children. As my athletes work with the youngsters, I always venture outside fenced-in courts and engage in conversation with some of the adults. On one particular occasion, I introduced myself to Renaldo, a handsome young man who said he was 18 years old. He was sitting on a rock watching the activity. I invited him to participate, but he was shy. I sat down beside him and proceeded to tell him why we were there. I shared the gospel while the bugs in nearby bushes literally ate me up. He listened, and he told me he needed a job. I prayed with him and took him to meet some of the players. He hung out with us most of the afternoon.

On another occasion I was witnessing to another man when a woman came up and began listening. She told me she had Jesus in her heart, but she didn't know if she would go to heaven when she died. I proceeded to show her in the Bible, beginning with John 3:16, how she could know for sure, and then I prayed with her. She went away rejoicing that she knew she would go to heaven. There are many other stories of people "outside the courts" who just come to watch but find Jesus through a divine appointment with one of our team members.

> The simplicity of the gospel has given me confidence in sharing Christ.

THE GOSPEL ~ KEEP IT SIMPLE

I am a great admirer of evangelist Billy Graham and his ministry. When the final history is written on the twentieth century, I am confident that Dr. Graham will have impacted more lives throughout the world than any other person. I believe history will record him as the most influential person of the century. For years, I have marveled at the success of his campaigns and the numbers of people professing Christ following his services.

He always kept the gospel message simple. He never wavered or changed the message, and he never dressed it up with theology. He took the simplicity of John 3:16 and called the world into a relationship with God through His Son, Jesus Christ. I have chosen to use this verse in my sports evangelism ministry and in my own personal life when sharing the gospel. Through the years I have taken courses on how to share the gospel, memorizing Scripture and outlines that required a lot of study and practice. All that has served me well, but realizing the simplicity of the gospel has given me the confidence and ease in sharing Christ that I had looked for all my life. My decision to adopt this verse was solidified while I was on a missions trip to Rio, Brazil. During the orientation, the missionary gave me an outline for witnessing. It was basically John 3:16. It works for me, plain and simple, year after year, as I adapt it to the situation at hand. Here is a synopsis:

G O D ~ loves you. He has a plan for your life...and He wants to have a relationship with you—now and forever.

S I N ~ separates us from God. The Bible says all of us have sinned.

J E S U S ~ But, God loved us so much that He sent His Son, Jesus, to die on the Cross for our sin (see John 3:16).

B E L I E V E and C O N F E S S and T R U S T ~ If we believe that Jesus died for our sin, and if we confess our sin and ask Him to forgive us, and trust Him to do what He said He would do...

H E A V E N ~ He will forgive us, live in our hearts, and give us the free gift of eternal life.

I N V I T A T I O N ~ Would you like to ask Jesus to forgive you of your sin...invite Him into your heart and life...and trust Him for the free gift of eternal life? Would you like to do this right now? You can repeat a prayer like this one after me.

P R A Y E R ~ *Lord Jesus, I know I am a sinner. I believe You died on the Cross for my sin. Forgive me of my sin; come into my heart and be my Lord and Savior...and give me the free gift of eternal life. Thank You, Jesus, for forgiving me of my sin and for the promise of being with You in heaven forever.*

F O L L O W - U P ~ You have just made the most important decision of your life. You now have a relationship with God through His Son, Jesus Christ, and that relationship can never be taken away from you. And, the Bible says that because you have Jesus in your heart, when you die you will go to heaven to live with Him for eternity!

To continue to grow, you should:
1. Find a church with like-minded believers and attend regularly.
2. Read the Bible. It is your instruction book for life.
3. Pray to God every day. As you talk with Him, your relationship will deepen.

THE FACE OF AN ANGEL

When I think about why I share the gospel I remember back to a Sunday morning in Tarnow, Poland, in 1997. We were concluding the worship service with Communion. I was filming the service with a video camera when I was captivated by a woman's face. She was old, her features worn, but she had the face of an angel.

I watched as she took the cup, drank from it, and placed it back into the plate. She began to pray quietly. Tears flowed down her cheeks as she put her face in her hands and wept. I stopped filming, lowered the camera, and stared at the woman. We made a connection beyond my comprehension; it was a powerful moment for me. She continued to observe the Lord's Supper when the bread was passed.

I dropped my head and reflected on what I had just witnessed. I was drawn to this woman's obvious communion with Christ and her personal identity with the Cross. Was this the real meaning of Communion? If so, I had been missing the mark all these years.

I could hardly wait to meet her after the service. She greeted me with a smile, tears and words flowing out in Polish. I tried to communicate with her with my tears, my gestures, and my love. A Polish student came to translate. I told the woman that I had observed her during Communion, and God had spoken to me through her. She told me she was 90 years old, had been through two world wars, lost all her family, and spent time in the work camps during the second war. She said Jesus is the reason for her being alive today. He had brought her through much pain, suffering, fear, and tragedy.

"Thank you for coming," she said. "Tell my people about Jesus. He is our only hope."

As her tears flowed, I gently held her face in my hands, this face of an angel. She placed her hands on my cheeks. We held one another tightly, drawn together by the blood of Jesus. I called for the college athletes who were traveling with me to come meet her. They, too, responded with hugs and genuine love and affection. I don't need that video to remind me of her face.

> "Tell my people about Jesus. He is our only hope."

I ask myself, what do people see when they look into my face? Does it give a testimony of what Christ has done in my life?

In Acts 8:26–40 we read of Philip and the Ethiopian eunuch. Verse 34 says: "The eunuch asked Philip, 'Tell me, please, who is the prophet talking about...' Then Philip...told him the good news about Jesus."

I have written in my Bible beside verse 34: "Betty...tell me, please!" When I read this verse I think about the "face of an angel" and her cry, "Tell my people about Jesus. He is our only hope."

CALLED AND ACCOUNTABLE

B ut in your hearts set apart Christ as Lord. Always be prepared to give an answer to everyone who asks you to give the reason for the hope that you have" (1 Peter 3:15).

We had just completed a long morning's sports ministry in Rio Des Padres, a slum in Rio, Brazil. It was noon and our team of athletes went to an enclosed area for lunch—beans and rice and canned soda. It was a welcomed reprieve from the hot sun, mosquitoes, and crowds. I was tired from the heat, hungry, and ready for food; I selected a chair somewhat removed from the others. All I wanted was to sit still, eat, be quiet, and rest. Before I took my first bite, I heard my name, "Beh-Chi, (Betty in Portuguese), someone wants to see you outside."

Somewhat irritated that my lunch and rest time had been interrupted, I left the room. Outside with the crowd there stood a woman who looked to be in her 50s. She said to me through a translator, "My friend came to my house and told me to go see Beh-Chi, the American, to learn about Jesus. Will you tell me about Jesus?"

She listened carefully for the next 20 or 30 minutes as I shared the good news with her. "God loves you and has a plan for your life, and He wants to have a relationship with you. However, sin in our lives separates us from God. But, the Bible says in John 3:16 that God loved you so much that He sent His one and only Son, Jesus, to die on the Cross for your sin. If you believe that Jesus died on the Cross for your sin, if you will ask Him to forgive you of your sin and trust Him to forgive you, He will come into your heart and live in your heart forever. And, He will give you the free gift of eternal life. You can do that right now by praying a short prayer with me. I can help you say that prayer. Do you want to ask Jesus into your heart?"

"Yes," she replied, "I believe what you say about Jesus, and I want Jesus in my heart."

Right then and there, this woman prayed with me to receive Christ!

"Thank you," she said. "I must go tell my friend that I have Jesus in my heart too."

She went away rejoicing. My heart was filled with joy. My lunchtime was nearly over, but I was no longer hungry. I was filled up and overflowing. "My food," said Jesus "is to do the will of him who sent me and to finish his work" (John 4:34). I don't even remember finishing my lunch. The morning's fatigue was gone, and I was more than ready for the rest of the day's ministry. There were others waiting to hear the good news of Jesus' love. I had more to do!

Nothing, absolutely nothing, compares to leading someone in a prayer to receive Christ! We must always be prepared, whether we're on a missions trip to Brazil or in our neighborhood. Interruptions in our daily lives just might be divine appointments.

SOWING SEEDS

Growing up on a farm in Tennessee, I enjoyed rural life, and I loved working with my dad in the fields. I was the ultimate farm girl. There was nothing about farm work that I did not like, so I looked forward to whatever the day's work would bring. There was no sitting still during the light of day, and there were always things to do.

I remember being intrigued in the springtime when I watched my dad sow seeds by hand. He carried the seeds in a special bag, hanging from his shoulder. He walked the fields in a slow, steady gait, carefully reaching in and out of the bag, gathering a handful of seed, and then spreading the seed with a smooth and gentle, almost rhythmical, motion. The seed always fell evenly. How could he do that? As a little girl, I often followed him, stepping in his footsteps, pretending I was spreading seeds too.

Then Dad watched for storms, worrying over his seed, trusting they would have a chance to take root before winds or heavy rains washed them away. They needed just the right amount of light rain to soak them into the ground that had been so carefully prepared.

I vividly remember him standing on our front porch at night looking at the sky, watching and waiting, probably praying for his seed.

> We are to sow the seeds, allowing the Holy Spirit to water and nourish them.

We are called as Christians to sow seeds in our daily lives wherever God has placed us. He calls us to walk in His footsteps and sow seeds of joy, hope, kindness, gentleness, peace, faith, love, and forgiveness. And, He tells us to sow these seeds with gentleness and great care. Do we? Or, do we go our own way and carelessly drop seeds of jealousy, hurt, strife, pain, and anger? The Bible says that some of our seeds will fall on deaf ears or hard ground and never take root, but we don't have to worry about that. We are to sow the seeds, allowing the Holy Spirit to water and nourish them. We don't always see the fruits of our labor. We are told that some people will sow and others will reap. "Thus the saying 'One sows and another reaps' is true" (John 4:37).

I think about those formative years of my life on the farm when I learned many life lessons. My earthly father taught me how to sow seed for my heavenly Father; with gentleness, respect, love, and great care.

OBEDIENCE

To use popular phrases: Jesus was a "man of action," a "mover and a shaker." He was not content to sit around. He went about preaching, teaching, healing, feeding the hungry, raising the dead, shepherding, comforting, and praying. Crowds flocked to see and hear Him. Some climbed trees to get a glimpse while others made their way to rooftops. People got to Him any way they could. Today He might be called a radical. He taught in parables, causing people to think. Imagine that! He was persecuted, tried as a criminal, scorned, beaten, and crucified on a cross. In His last moments on the Cross,

He responded to the request of one of the criminals hanging next to Him: "Today you shall be with me in paradise." He even asked the Father to "forgive them for they know not what they do."

John, in his Gospel, tells us that if someone wrote down everything Jesus did, the world itself could not contain the books that would have to be written. "Jesus did many other things as well. If every one of them were written down, I suppose that even the whole world would not have room for the books that would be written" (John 21:25). And this testimony comes from an eyewitness, someone who knew Jesus for at least three years.

Jesus said, "My Father is always at his work to this very day, and I, too, am working" (John 5:17). I personalized this Scripture in my Bible by writing, "Betty, too, shall be at work." It is a reminder that I am to be obedient, to be "on mission" every day. Jesus asked His followers to pray for more workers because the fields were already overflowing and ripe for harvest. There were things to do, and He knew He would not be physically present to do them.

Are we imitators of Christ? Are we people of action? Are we doing, or are we sitting in the church pews just being a sponge? Jesus took action! He was obedient, even unto death.

If, at death, an eyewitness were to write an account of your life and what you did for Jesus, what would he say and how long would the account of your actions be? I pray that God would find us all faithful, that we would all be obedient in doing His work, and that it would be in response to all He has done for us.

Just Do It

I was 11 years old when I asked Jesus into my heart. I remember it as if it were yesterday! I could not wait for the next day of school so I could tell someone. I told my teacher. I was excited, and it was good news worth sharing. Today, I can't wait until the next time I have an opportunity to share the good news of Jesus' love.

I have been given an awesome platform for sharing this good news. My decades of teaching and coaching experiences have prepared me for my passion of sharing Christ. But going and telling is a real challenge. It is a risk that takes us outside our comfort zone, requiring total dependence on God. It is faith that throws fear of failure to the wind. Diving off that platform brings a new freedom in Christ, a freeing up of oneself to ministry. Making that initial dive is the challenge. You may even need a push by someone who believes in you and your gifts and abilities.

There is urgency, more than ever before, to tell the nations. There is work to do! We have been entrusted with the gospel (1 Thessalonians 2:4), and we have been equipped with the armor of God (Ephesians 6:10–18). I have learned some principles of evangelism and collected a wealth of personal stories, all because I dove off the platform and into ministry.

Here are some promises I have claimed as an "on-mission" Christian. These are promises that have spoken to me and have become my own personal armor. I am confident they will support you also. God's Word, when spoken in love, does not come back void.

"For God did not give us a spirit of timidity, but a spirit of power, of love and of self-discipline."

~ 2 TIMOTHY 1:7

"The Lord stood at my side and gave me strength, so that through me the message might be fully proclaimed."

~ 2 TIMOTHY 4:17

"I am not ashamed of the gospel, because it is the power
of God for the salvation of everyone who believes."
~ ROMANS 1:16

"Whatever you do, work at it with all your heart, as
working for the Lord, not for men...It is the
Lord Christ you are serving."
~ COLOSSIANS 3:23–24

"My grace is sufficient for you, for my power is
made perfect in weakness."
~ 2 CORINTHIANS 12:9

"Do not worry about what to say or how to say it. At that
time you will be given what to say, for it will not be you
speaking, but the Spirit of your Father
speaking through you."
~ MATTHEW 10:19–20

"But you are a chosen people, a royal priesthood, a holy
nation, a people belonging to God, that you may declare
the praises of him who called you out of darkness
into his wonderful light."
~ 1 PETER 2:9

"But you will receive power when the Holy Spirit comes
on you; and you will be my witnesses in Jerusalem, and
in all Judea and Samaria, and to the ends of the earth."
~ ACTS 1:8

Confidence and competence in ministry, including evangelism, is ours through Christ. It comes from God. "He has made us competent as ministers of a new covenant" (2 Corinthians 3:4–6). Missions must become who we are; not what we do in everyday life! Personalize Colossians 4:17 for yourself. *"Tell* (insert your name): 'See to it that you complete the work you have received in the Lord.'"

I challenge you to take the plunge. Just do it. Take action. Sow the seeds of the gospel. It is a risk worth taking! It will change your life!

CHAPTER 2

DIVINE APPOINTMENTS

One of my favorite Bible stories is found in the fourth chapter of John: Jesus meeting the Samaritan woman at Jacob's well. Jesus asked the woman, "Will you give me a drink?" She responded, "You are a Jew and I am a Samaritan woman. How can you ask me for a drink?" (John 4:7–9). Jesus went on to share with her that He is the Living Water. Ultimately, because of this seemingly "chance" encounter with Jesus, not only did she believe, but also many other Samaritans believed after hearing her testimony.

This story took on even more meaning for me when my pastor, Mike Glenn, preached on it recently. He noted verses 3–4, "He [Jesus] left Judea and went back once more to Galilee. Now he had to go through Samaria." Did Jesus really have to go through Samaria from Judea to get to Galilee? Pastor Glenn made the point that Jesus could or probably would have gone another route except for the fact that there was a divine appointment waiting for Him at Jacob's well. That point registered with me because of so many divine appointments I have had along the way on my overseas missions trips. And, I have noticed divinely orchestrated appointments await me most days in my work and play here in Nashville; I just need to be in tune with the Father's will and leadership in my life.

A SIMPLE PRAYER

I was in Warsaw, Poland, with a team of basketball players, men and women. Our ministry consisted of working in the Polish schools in the mornings, conducting basketball clinics in the afternoons, and playing Polish club teams in the evenings.

While in the classrooms, students asked why we were there. This opened doors for us to share who Jesus Christ is and how to have a personal relationship with Him. They were curious about the word *personal* in our faith, our religion. They had never heard of a personal Savior or personal relationship. Most of them listened, although some were antagonistic, trying to get attention.

Left to right: Peter, Michael, Thom.

There were three of us in a classroom, sharing conversation. I noticed three young guys who were listening attentively. Later, as we spent time outside on the school grounds in small groups, one of our team members motioned for me to join him and three boys. There were the three guys that I had noticed in the classroom: Peter, Thom, and Michael. I sat down as Michael told us about his girlfriend who was in the hospital in a coma. She had been in a car wreck, and the doctor told her family she probably would not make it. Only a miracle could save her.

I said, "Why don't we pray for her?"

"Right here?" they replied. "How can we do that?"

They had grown up in a Catholic home, and they were accustomed to going through their priest with prayers.

"Yes, here," I said. "You see, you can pray here, or anywhere, at any time. God hears our prayers wherever we are. He is with us right here. I want to pray for your girlfriend now. I don't know her, but God does. He will hear us."

They looked around, kind of anxious about praying, but they said yes. We bowed our heads, and I prayed for this young girl; for healing and for God's will to be done in her life. When I finished my prayer, they listened as I shared how to have a personal relationship with Christ. They were nice young men, courteous, kind, and interested. We invited them to our Thursday night evangelistic service at the school auditorium. They promised to come.

That night as our team warmed up for the exhibition game with a local team I saw Thom walking across the gym floor toward me.

"Betty, Betty, I have good news," Thom shouted as he approached me.

"What is it, Thom?" I replied, instantly thinking of the girl I had prayed for.

"Michael sent me to tell you his girlfriend came out of the coma. The doctor said she will recover and that it is a miracle."

"That's wonderful, Thom. I am so happy." I was smiling inside and thanking God.

"And, guess what time she came out of the coma!" he beamed. "It was the exact time you prayed for her this afternoon. Michael said to tell you thank you."

"God answered our prayer, Thom. Tell Michael to thank God, not me."

As he turned to walk away I said, "See you Thursday night."

"We will be there," he replied.

They came Thursday night, and they heard more about God's love for all people of the world. They heard how much He loved us, by sending His one and only Son, Jesus, to die on the Cross for our sin. They heard the gospel, shared by our team through music, drama, and the spoken word. When the invitation came for people to respond, Peter, Thom, and Michael were ready to give their hearts to Christ. Those three boys became my brothers in Christ that night. God used a prayer in an unlikely place, under the shade of a tree in a schoolyard in Warsaw, Poland, to reveal Himself in a miraculous way. It was a divine appointment. I have underlined John 4:53 in my Bible with the words written beside it to remind me: Poland '95—Peter, Thom, Michael. "Then the father realized that this was the exact time at which Jesus had said to him, 'Your son will live.' So he and all his household believed."

> God used a prayer in an unlikely place to reveal Himself in a miraculous way.

A framed photograph in my home of Peter, Thom, Michael, and me serves as another reminder of that appointment and the power of prayer.

Agnes's Change of Heart

And then there was Agnes, from that same class, who had chosen to be somewhat antagonistic, snickering and making fun during the first class session. Initially, I was a little irritated with her disruptiveness during class, but then I realized I had seen students like this through the years in my own classes. Before class ended, I challenged her to come Thursday night to the evangelistic service—just come and listen, see what she thought. She came, brought some friends, and listened. The next day we were back in the same classroom for follow-up. I noticed her demeanor was different. She didn't interrupt or talk or seek attention. She was listening.

I said to the class, "Some of you were with us last night. What did you think?"

As students asked questions and we engaged in dialogue, I kept my eyes open to Agnes. Finally, she spoke.

"I came last night. It did something to me. I don't know what it all means, but I want to know more," she said as big tears ran down her cheeks.

"I know what it is, Agnes. Come with me and we'll talk."

I took her out of the classroom, into the hallway, and found an old wooden bench where we sat. We talked a while about what she was feeling. I shared the gospel and answered some questions she had. I said, "Do you want to ask Jesus into your heart?"

"Yes, I do," she replied with a big smile.

I proceeded to lead her as she prayed to receive Christ, right there on that old wooden bench, in the dark hallway of a Polish high school. God had revealed Himself to yet another student in a most unusual place.

When we finished I said, "Agnes, when you die what will happen to you?"

"I will go to heaven to live forever," she said with a smile as big as the sun.

"How do you know that?" I asked.

"Because I have asked Jesus to forgive me of my sins and to live in my heart," she replied.

"Agnes, when I leave Poland I may never see you again on this earth, but we will see one another again someday in heaven. You are my sister in Christ."

We walked downstairs where many people had gathered between classes. Our team could tell by the smiles on our faces what had happened. I introduced Agnes to our team as our new sister in Christ. There were lots of hugs and tears of celebration for Agnes. I was flooded with joy.

Absolutely nothing compares with leading someone to salvation in Christ Jesus. All those big wins and celebrations and championships and awards I had as a basketball coach become very small and insignificant when compared to the victory of leading someone to Christ. I am confident that when I stand before God at the end of my journey, He won't ask how many trophies I brought with me. But He will ask how many people I brought with me.

UNEXPECTED DELAY

A delay in Pittsburgh on our second trip to Poland caused us to miss our Polish Air flight out of Newark that evening. However, it provided us with a glimpse of God's "unexpected blessings" that would be afforded us through the trip. A complete stranger on the sidewalk at the nearly deserted airport recommended a motel that might have enough room for all of us; and yes, they did. It took five cabs to get us and our loads of luggage over to the motel. Finally, after a frustrating two hours, we settled in for our delay. We were happy to all be together, even if we were in a strange place with piles of luggage. In addition to our luggage, we had three big boxes containing a computer and all the accessories for the missionaries awaiting us in Poland.

A call back to Nashville put us in touch with Southern Baptist home missionaries, Nancy and DeLane Ryals, who just happened to live ten miles from our Newark motel. A late-night conversation with them provided us a promise of safe passage the following day to the airport for an evening flight, 24 hours behind schedule. The Ryals were the parents of two daughters who were Belmont graduates, both of whom were my former students. Another unexpected blessing came the next day when the Ryals gave us a two-hour tour and history lesson—which included the Statue

> I fought back the tears of gratitude, and thanked God that He was in control and not me.

of Liberty and Ellis Island—before taking us to the airport. Not one of our team had ever been to New York or New Jersey, much less seen the Statue of Liberty.

We arrived in Warsaw a day late and began our ministry in a local high school. We first visited an English class. The teacher handed me a page, torn from a book. On the page was a picture of the Statue of Liberty.

She said, "We are studying about the Statue of Liberty and would like for you to tell us about it and give us your impressions of it."

I wanted to fall on my knees before God as I took the picture, but I smiled and graciously said, "We would be happy to share with you. We have just come from there."

The team began to share with great enthusiasm and excitement. I found a seat in the rear of the classroom, fought back the tears of gratitude, and thanked God that He was in control and not me. We now knew why we had missed our plane in Newark. It was another divine appointment, orchestrated by God, so that we would be appropriately prepared to respond to a request by that first classroom visit.

SETH MEETS JESUS

Seth met Jesus on our second trip to Poland in 1996. He was the last member to join our team for the trip. He was a special young man with a beautiful heart, quiet, introspective, and he loved to read. He was a gentle young man with a sensitive nature and sweet spirit. He told me of his desire to be a part of a missions team.

"I love people," he said. "I want to make a difference in this world by doing something like this."

I wasn't exactly sure of the depth of Seth's faith. I spend a lot of time observing athletes, praying, asking God to help me in the make-up of each missions team. God really put Seth on my heart that year, so I invited him to go with us to Poland.

Something happened to Seth on that trip. The youth were especially drawn to him. Everywhere we went, he had followers. And, he and Voitek, a Polish seminary student who translated for us, spent a lot of time together. I would discover upon return to the States that Seth gave his heart to Christ one night at the seminary after several long conversations with Voitek. He said he thought he was a Christian, but realized while he was in Poland that he had never fully committed himself to Christ. God used an unlikely person in an unlikely place to influence a Belmont athlete to give his heart to Christ. It was a divine appointment for Seth.

During the Christmas holidays the following December, I received a call at my home to tell me that Seth had been found dead in a field, at the base of a radio tower, not far from his home. He had fallen while attempting to climb the tower. No one knows why Seth had attempted this feat. He had been missing several hours. When they found him, his dog was sitting by his side, guarding his body.

The news of his death broke my heart and shocked our campus. I, along with coaches, teammates, and others from Belmont, attended his funeral. My heart ached, and I struggled with my thoughts and emotions. Seth had come back from the trip to Poland a changed man. He spent countless hours reading the Bible and searching for answers

The 1996 missions trip to Poland was a divine appointment for Seth Pettus.

to lots of questions. He was like a sponge absorbing things he was discovering.

I remembered getting a call from him, asking me to meet him in a local park to talk. It was in September following the trip in May. I was eager to accommodate. He told me of his conversion experience in Poland and thanked me for taking him on the trip. He asked me questions, deep and probing questions. He wanted to give up everything and follow Christ. Following Christ had taken the place of basketball as the focus in his life. We talked a long time. I prayed with Seth before leaving the park that day, told him I loved him, and how happy I was that he had found Christ on the trip to Poland. I will always cherish that special time in the park with Seth in late September 1996.

I don't know all that was going on in Seth's mind and heart. But I know this one thing: it was God's leading that caused me to ask Seth on that trip to Poland. He was headed for a divine appointment with Jesus. I believe Seth is in heaven today, and has met Jesus face-to-face because he was on that missions trip. I can't wait to see Seth again. He will have all the answers to his questions, and we can rejoice in the presence of God, the God he came to know personally in Poland.

THERE'S A PARTY GOING ON!

Missionaries Paul and Shelley Scott's two youngest children, Sydney (then 10) and Josey (then 8), came with their mom and dad to the airport in Caracas to greet our missions team when we arrived in Venezuela in 2006. They soon became family. Their oldest son, Jordan, then a student at Union University in Tennessee, also joined us a few days later in La Cruz. It was a special treat to spend time with the entire Scott family.

Josey and Sydney were with us for evenings the first few days and then joined us on Saturday morning as we traveled to Anaco and La Cruz for the second week of work. Josey was everywhere! He loved playing with the basketballs and enjoyed riding in the vans with our guys. He thought he was just as big and helpful in ministry as the college athletes. And, he bonded with a lot of kids in the crowds and ran relays every day. Bedtime came easy for him as he exhausted himself during the day.

> "Miss Betty, I just got saved. I asked Jesus into my heart."

Sometimes when I'm sharing the gospel I use Revelation 3:20 where Jesus says, "I stand at the door and knock. If anyone hears my voice and opens the door, I will come in." Paul told us one morning that he had asked Josey if God was knocking at the door of his heart. Josey responded, "I think he is going to." Nothing else was said.

It was Monday afternoon, and we had just finished two sessions that day in two different schools. Many people had just prayed to trust Christ. Then we had a time of mingling, hanging out, and signing autographs. Someone pointed out Paul and Shelley sitting under a nearby tree with Josey; they were talking and praying. I was sitting in a chair watching our athletes and talking with students. All at once, two little arms circled my neck from behind the chair, and this little voice said, "Miss Betty, I just got saved. I asked Jesus into my heart." It was Josey! I pulled him into my lap and hugged him tight. He told me he asked Jesus into his heart when we shared the gospel with the large group. It was a special moment! Josey had heard us share the gospel and give invitations several times before. Of course, we were all excited for our "littlest" teammate.

The next day Shelley said she asked Josey if Jesus was still in his heart. He responded, "Of course! There's a party going on in my heart."

You just can't put it better than that!

While in La Cruz we worked with another missionary couple on Tuesday night and all day Wednesday before completing our ministry. The Scotts got a phone call on Tuesday night from this couple saying that their 10-year-old son also had prayed that day with the crowd to receive Christ. I found out later that Josey Scott had asked the boy prior to the session if he had Jesus in his heart. Josey had told him, "All you got to do is believe, say a prayer, and invite Him in."

Pretty simple, huh? We make it so complex. The Bible says, "A little child will lead them" (Isaiah 11:6). "There's a party going on in my heart!" I love that simple statement of faith!

Missionaries Paul and Shelley Scott
and their children, Sydney, Josey and Jordan.

Keaton Belcher helps
missionary kid Josey
Scott dunk the ball.

WOW MOMENTS!

GONZALO AND YINNA

Gonzalo was four years old, the son of the church caretaker for El Sembrador Baptist Church in Temuco, Chile. Gonzalo had big beautiful eyes and a smile as wide as the ocean. His head was covered with black curly locks that framed the cutest face I believe I'd ever seen. He was beautiful! He was always at our after-school activities, and loved trying to bounce the basketballs I had brought with me to use as I worked and played with the kids. He would sit with me during the church services on Sundays. He was everywhere, and most certainly had found a place in my heart. He became Betty's special little boy.

Yinna [Gina] had been at the airport with her aunt and others from the church to greet our team on my initial trip to Chile in August 1992. She was six years old, and for some reason she found me as I came into the airport upon our arrival. As our team retrieved our bags, Yinna took my hand and held it until we parted for our destination. She appeared again and again through those ten days, sitting with

Betty, Gonzalo, and Gina were almost inseparable during the 1992 missions trip to Chile.

me, holding my hand, or standing by my side. When I returned to Chile in October for an extended stay, Yinna was there again. She joined Gonzalo on the pew beside me for worship each Sunday. Yinna became Betty's special little girl.

Betty with her two Chilean children, Gonzalo and Yinna

A Sunday night worship service sealed my friendship with these two children. The pastor had called the church to prayer. Now, when people in Chile are called to prayer, they kneel at the altar. It is always a powerful and very meaningful time in each service. I was at the altar, on my knees in prayer, when I felt a tug at my left side, and this little hand wrapped around my left arm. I peeped around and saw Gonzalo was kneeling beside me, looking up into my face. Tears ran down my cheeks as I took his hand. Then I felt another tug on my right. Yinna, on her knees, taking my right hand. There I was at the altar with my two Chilean children, joining me in prayer. That was a WOW moment for me. It was also an affirmation from God as to why I was there. Gonzalos and Yinnas are all over the world waiting for someone to love them through Christ.

OPENING NEW DOORS

In May 2000, I led a team to work with a missionary couple, Steve and Sharon Ford, in Portugal. It was their first-ever attempt at sports evangelism in the country. They had no clue what sports evangelism was or how it worked. They had only heard secondhand about our ministry.

We were told in orientation, prior to the trip, that the people of Portugal would not be open to the gospel, that it would be difficult to get into places and connect with the people. We were told to expect to "plant seeds." I prayed that we would be faithful in planting seeds, and I prayed fervently that I would be bold and look for opportunities daily to bring someone to Christ.

The Fords shared with us that the doors to the schools had never been open to the missionaries before. They had tried to rent the school facilities for church and community activities, but they were always turned down. They also shared that their recognition and acceptance within the community had been nonexistent. It wasn't the Portuguese culture to be friendly, speak, or offer greetings to outsiders. Actually, the Fords had become discouraged in their work.

As our trip went on, it was exciting to watch them bond with our athletes and become more and more comfortable with our strategy. We were able to go to two schools and do our presentations.

Following our visits, both principals gave the Fords open invitations to return any time they so desired. The school doors were now open to them. The second school offered their facilities to the church and community, free of charge, at any time. The Fords called this a miracle. Soon, they began getting friendly hellos in their community.

One night Steve Ford went into a local grocery, following a day of our ministry, and someone yelled, "Hey, Pastor. Where are your Americans?" I can't tell you the joy on Steve's face when he told of someone recognizing him and calling out to him. He also told about being on a train one night going to a meeting and seeing a young man with a Belmont basketball jersey and John 3:16 printed in Portuguese on the back. There are lots of those jerseys on the kids' backs in Portugal. People will pay attention and read. God will do the rest!

Wow! God continues to wow me! He takes ordinary people, puts us in unfamiliar places, and does extraordinary things. He taught us so much while in Portugal. It was a new country, and we were not easily accepted. However, sports evangelism opened doors that had always been closed. Missionaries now know that sports is a mighty tool for sharing Christ. And, people are receptive to the gospel in Portugal. It may just depend on the "platform" for sharing the good news of Jesus Christ!

OUTSIDE THE FENCE

A team from Belmont was in Zhitomir, Ukraine, in 2005 when one day following lunch we drove back to the park where we had ministered the afternoon before. Our team was physically and emotionally drained from playing all morning with the street kids. But as we drove up there were dozens of kids from the previous day waiting for their American friends to play. I stopped the bus and requested we sit still, be quiet, and rest for 15 minutes. I reminded the team that Jesus often retreated to a quiet place, away from the crowds, to rest. I encouraged them to close their eyes and take what I call a "power nap." Most of the team dozed off as I rested and waited for the moment to wake them up and renew our focus.

And, what an afternoon awaited us! It was filled with more play and more one-to-one and small-group sharing. I shared Christ with two girls who prayed to receive Him. I noticed five young boys standing close by and listening. They were waiting for their turn. I immediately turned my attention to these 10- or 11-year-olds and shared the gospel with them. All five invited Jesus into their hearts. What a wonderful experience for me. The day came to a climax with a large sit-down session for sharing the gospel through drama, testimonies, and an invitation to receive Christ. Fifty or more people prayed to ask Jesus into their hearts in a powerful demonstration of the Holy Spirit. It was a God-ordained moment in our trip.

Following the session, a team member pointed out to me three women with babies outside the fenced-in-court. She said they had wandered off the street and had listened through the fence. I immediately went outside the court to them and asked if they understood what we had said. They said they understood. I asked if they would like to ask Jesus into their hearts and their response was, "We already have. We prayed with the children." They received Christ that day as they wandered down the street and stopped to listen through a fence to some Americans sharing the gospel with children. We never know how God will use us when we are bold enough to

Betty with a young woman who wanted to know Jesus.

stand up and profess His saving grace. It was a divine appointment!

As I recall this wow moment of triumph, I also recall the statement made to me prior to this particular trip that the Ukraine is closed to the gospel. The thought now makes me smile.

YOU ARE THE CHURCH

It was a Sunday morning in Rio, Brazil, May 2008, and our team of basketball players was scheduled for an exhibition and clinic with kids at a local sports club. I was uncomfortable with the schedule the missionaries had put together for a Sunday morning on a missions trip. We were scheduled to be in a local church that evening, because the evening service is considered the "big" Sunday service. I thought we should be going to a small local church to have an additional church experience that morning. But, I kept my thoughts to myself and got on the bus for the 30-minute drive to the club.

We walked into the gymnasium where some 200-plus kids of all ages awaited us, along with maybe that many or more parents and family members sitting in the stands. There they were, waiting for some basketball time. We went into the locker rooms for last-minute preparation, and too soon, we heard the announcer begin the introductions. One by one, he called our names, and we ran out between lines of kids, clapping and lining up on the court as the crowd cheered for our entrance. It was a chilling and exhilarating moment. The game was on!

We proceeded to go through the routine—a warm-up, exhibition of skills and drills, a short intrasquad exhibition game, and then into drills, games, and relays with the kids. The crowd loved the action and responded with cheers. They were connected to the moment. This went on for about two hours.

It was time to have the kids sit down for our testimonies and sharing of the gospel. All of a sudden, God spoke to me and said, *"Betty, this is church for you today. It isn't what you are used to on a Sunday morning or what you may have expected, but this is my divine appointment for you this morning to share the gospel."*

I was overcome with God's presence and His divine leadership as I directed the kids and young people to come sit on the floor right in front of their families. I took the microphone, asked the families to move closer together, and invited them to listen to our message. An incredible hush came over that place and our church service began.

A couple of our players gave greetings and testimonies and a perfect lead-in to the gospel. I stood before the "church" seated in that gymnasium and spoke to all who sat before me about God's love and the amazing saving grace of Jesus Christ. It was one of the most powerful and spirit-filled moments I have ever experienced. They listened intently as I shared how to have a relationship with Jesus Christ and what that would mean in their lives. The invitation to receive Christ was a joyous occasion as men, women, boys, and girls prayed with me in faith. I can still see that crowd and hear the sound of their voices as I led them in English through a translator, and they prayed in Portuguese. My heart soars with praise when I even think about it.

> God spoke to me and said, "Betty, this is church for you today."

Several parents came up to me afterwards and thanked me for the message and the opportunity we had given them. One couple approached me to say thank you. I asked them, "Are you believers? Do you have Jesus in your heart?"

The man replied, "I am, but my wife is not," acknowledging her with a smile.

I looked at her and said, "What are you waiting for?"

"I don't know," she said. "I am interested. I guess I'm waiting for something big to happen."

I proceeded to talk with her and finally said, "Maybe today is the 'something big' you are looking for. You know, we came all the way from the United States to share this message with you. That's pretty big, isn't it?" She smiled and nodded her head.

Finally, I said, "Don't you want to reconsider and invite Jesus into your heart to be your Lord and Savior?"

"Yes, I do," she replied. And, she did, right then and there! She cried, she laughed, and she hugged, celebrating as her husband embraced her. They made pictures of us together, and I gave her a New Testament with a handwritten message from me commemorating her "birthday" in Christ.

Our time was up, and it was difficult leaving that place. As we pulled away, I stood on the bus and confessed to the team, missionaries, and translators my feelings prior to the ministry. It was a lesson learned

Betty enjoyed playing with the children in Rio.

worth sharing, a teachable moment. God had shown me, *"Betty, never underestimate what I can do. You are 'the church' wherever you are if you are willing to stand and proclaim the good news of Jesus Christ. My ways are not your ways and My timing is not your timing."*

That morning was another divine appointment, and it will forever be a defining moment in my ministry!

CHAPTER 3

COMPASSION

Take a walk through the Gospels, one by one, and you will see how Jesus showed compassion for the people around Him. He identified with the needs of the people. In Matthew 9:36 we find, "When he saw the crowds, he had compassion on them, because they were harassed and helpless, like sheep without a shepherd." In Mark 8:1–2, we read, "Jesus called his disciples to him and said, 'I have compassion for these people.'" We are told in Colossians 3:12, "Therefore, as God's chosen people, holy and dearly loved, clothe your selves with compassion, kindness, humility, gentleness and patience."

The American College Dictionary defines compassion as "a feeling of sorrow or pity for the sufferings or misfortunes of another." One who is compassionate is sympathetic to the needs of others, responding to those needs with tenderness, kindness, love, care, and mercy. The ability to identify with and enter into a connection with others' needs is a gift from God. I believe it is born out of humility: an honest confession that without God I am nothing, and without God directing my life I am useless. Allowing God control of one's very being leads to a modest sense of one's own significance. And that ultimately leads us to put others first, entering into oneness with the pain, suffering, and needs of others. In this chapter, I'd like to share some stories that, for me, sum up what compassion is all about.

LAY YOUR TROPHIES DOWN

In what is now a long-standing tradition, I always host, in my home, the last sports evangelism team meeting prior to our overseas departure. Some students come early to fish in the lake out back. Others arrive following a final exam and crash on the patio. Mostly, they come for final instructions, to gather their uniforms and equipment to be packed, get a free home-cooked meal, and be encouraged and challenged as they approach departure.

It was May 2006, and we would be leaving the following Monday for Venezuela. We had finished our meal and had gathered in my living room. I shared with the team a detailed itinerary that I had just received from missionaries Paul and Shelley Scott. Even I was a bit overwhelmed when I saw the tentative schedule. It was obvious that God was going to get all He could from us during our time in Venezuela. We were scheduled for each morning, afternoon, and evening, and I saw no breaks in the schedule. Our free day for sightseeing and shopping was scheduled for the last day prior to coming home. It was going to be a very demanding schedule, but I was confident I had the perfect team to meet the challenge.

This particular team was made up primarily of male and female basketball players who had enjoyed the ultimate highs of conference championships and NCAA appearances. They had all been in the spotlight, on TV, in newspapers, and pretty much been on a pedestal. My personal challenge to them for this particular time was to lay their trophies down, put their accolades aside, and humble themselves before God for what He had called them to do. I shared this from Acts 21:19, 24: "I served the Lord with great humility and with tears... if only I may finish the race and complete the task the Lord Jesus has given me—the task of testifying to the gospel of God's grace."

Betty leads a couple in the sinner's prayer.

I spoke with certainty that there would be humbling moments on this trip when tears would be a testimony to what would be happening. I asked the group to begin their journey of humility right there, setting aside personal gains and focusing on the ministry opportunities before us. I shared from 2 Timothy 1:7: "For God did not give us a spirit of timidity, but a spirit of power, of love and of self-discipline."

Each team member found a place that night in my living room to kneel. In a spirit of deep humility, I led us in a prayer of commitment for the journey. They gathered their gear and departed.

I remember this experience so vividly because the team members had been quite successful in athletics while at Belmont, and I knew that their trophies would not be what would impress the people in Venezuela. In truth, every missions team needs this reminder. It is humility that is the starting point to loving others.

HUMBLED

I have never been humbled like I was in Zhitomir, Ukraine, in 2005. Our team was humbled to the very core of its being. We visited three different orphanages. We drove out of town and into a wooded area to the first orphanage. It was secluded and surrounded by woods. The large building that housed the orphans was institutional looking, very plain and uninviting. The youth began to appear from nowhere until we were surrounded by approximately 150 skeptical stares—that is until they spotted the bags of basketballs, volleyballs, and soccer balls. That turned their looks into friendly and inviting smiles. It didn't take long until the playground area turned into a beehive of activity.

The team from Belmont delivered treats to the orphanage.

Everybody was playing something or busy working with crafts. A circle gathered around some of our girls as they shared in making cross necklaces with colored beads. A makeshift table with concrete blocks for a net provided for a game of ping-pong. It was a hot afternoon and the mosquitoes were busy, especially with the Americans.

Children at the orphanage were eager to play basketball.

There were children of all ages, maybe 7 to 8 years old to 17 and 18 years. Most were frail, unkempt, dirty, hungry, and starved for attention. Clothes were makeshift, either too big or too small. We had to get used to the body odor, knowing some had not bathed in days. We saw only one adult the entire time we were there. It was summer break, and about half of the kids who lived in the area were gone somewhere for a few days. We touched, hugged, and loved, pouring out our hearts, and leaving a portion of ourselves with each child. I witnessed to two teenage girls who prayed to receive Christ, surrounded by the activity of play. We talked to one little guy, around 7 years old, who told us he was being adopted by Americans. He said his new mom and dad would come for him in three weeks. He had the biggest smile in the orphanage, and he had reason to smile. He told us his mommy and daddy's names were Karla and Steve. Oh, that there were more Karlas and Steves who would put smiles on faces of orphans by giving them a home and family.

Before we left, we gave them something to drink and then shared the gospel. Following testimonies, I told them how much God loved them and how He has a plan for each of their lives, and that God wants to have a relationship with them. I proceeded to tell them about Jesus and how each of them could ask Jesus into their hearts, how He could be their best friend. I gave them an opportunity to pray a prayer to receive Christ, and about 40 prayed the prayer out loud. God moved among dirt, filth, hunger, thirst, sadness, loneliness, and betrayal to give love, hope, forgiveness, living water, and eternal life. We left amid hugs, smiles, waves, and last-second touches of love. I remember specifically how drained we were emotionally, as well as physically, that night.

Two days later, we visited two more orphanages for ministry. It took quite a long time at the local market to buy $500 worth of food to distribute between the two places. This was our ticket to get in. We bought rice, noodles, sugar, and other staples, along with bananas, cookies, and candy for each child. In the first orphanage, we played outside on uneven dirt or in weeds and in a light rain. Finally, the rain forced us inside and cut short our time at the orphanage.

The second orphanage that day had the children seated in one large room where we talked to them, shared testimonies, and shared Christ. We did not get to play with them, but they were very receptive and open as we talked. Many prayed to receive Christ before we handed out the bananas, cookies, candy, and gifts. Not one of those children began eating, but held their goodies in their hands like treasures. The leaders told us they would take the bananas, cookies, candy, and gifts to their individual rooms and make them last as long as they could. They weren't greedy, just grateful. They walked out of the room and left us motionless and speechless. For a long time not one of us moved. Again, we were humbled and reminded that everything we have is by the grace of God.

Everyone listened intently to the Americans.

Love

The Mapuche Indians were Chile's first inhabitants. They now live on reservations, having received similar treatment as Native Americans of North America received. During one of my trips to Chile, I went with missionaries to a reservation to lead a worship service. It took us a long time to get there. The highway turned into gravel and then into dirt with potholes as deep as the wheels on the car. When the dirt road ended, we drove off into a field, headed toward a church building sitting on a hillside. The missionary families and I drove the only two cars. The Mapuches were waiting to greet us, and many were already inside. We saw more people coming out of the hills and surrounding mountains, walking toward the church.

The service was scheduled for 1:00 P.M. It wasn't just cold; it was really cold. There was no electricity; thus, no lights. The pews—long narrow logs—were packed with people. I was introduced as a visitor and asked to sing. There

Betty sang with the Mapuche Indians.

were no instruments, I thought, but I was used to singing spontaneously and a cappella. However, when I began to sing "How Great Thou Art" I heard music, not necessarily in the same key. A man was accompanying me with an old accordion. He struggled until he finally moved into the same key with me. Then God took over. The Indians were singing in Mapuche, the missionaries were singing in Spanish, and I was leading in English. I looked into their faces as they sang, and I saw God's love written all over them.

Our hearts were of one accord, and the Spirit of Christ filled the place. I shared with them afterwards how God's love is for the whole world, and I counted it a privilege to experience that love with them. I genuinely reached out in love to those people, as they did the same to me. With tears in my eyes, I said, "I love you. We can love one another because God first loved us."

I had about three layers of clothes on, plus a coat, gloves, and scarf around my neck, attempting to keep warm. I could see my breath as I sang and spoke. But, my heart was warm and cozy with God's love that filled the air.

Following the service, I hugged and spoke through a translator with many of the Mapuche. I gave my gloves to a little elderly lady who would be going back into the hills, wearing only a shabby old sweater for warmth. She didn't even know how to put them on. I had to demonstrate how to wear the gloves. The mental picture of that little church and the faces of those people will remain in my heart forever.

Speaking of cold, I had never experienced the cold anywhere like I did in Chile. It rains a lot, and the cold air coming from the mountains and snow-capped volcanoes chilled me to the bones. It was always a damp, penetrating, harsh cold. Most churches and homes had no heat. Babies and children wore so many layers that they waddled when they walked. I can remember times when I thought I just might freeze to death. It wasn't uncommon in homes where I visited for the people to place hot charcoal at my feet to keep me warm. But, I truly loved those people, and I found warmth in connecting with them through the love of Christ.

KINDNESS

Our team had just arrived in Puerto La Cruz, Venezuela, following a long afternoon drive from Anaco where we had spent the previous three days of our ministry. We checked into the hotel, changed clothes, and quickly made our way to a small fenced-in concrete court in the middle of a very poor neighborhood. It was surrounded by small homes, some mere shacks. People were everywhere, standing in doorways, mingling around, and staring. It was a new place; we had not adjusted to our new environment and felt rushed to get there. For the first time on the trip I felt a little uneasy.

I sensed a little uncertainty from the reception of some young men who waited to play. I just knew they were ready to compete with the Americans. It took a while and some real coaxing, but we finally broke the ice and had a pleasant time.

One young man in particular was anxious to compete and show his talents. He was somewhat uncooperative, so I accepted him as my challenge for the evening. It was obvious that he had an attitude problem. I could tell he was not about to relate to this older American woman in tennis shoes and shorts. I kept giving him extra attention; I worked on him all evening, and finally broke him down. He melted, gave in to my kindness, my smile and high fives, and we became friends.

We were sharing testimonies when a rain shower and darkness sent us to shelter. I was ready to share the gospel, but the rain prevented the completion of our sharing time. We were soaked as we made our way off the court. We took shelter in the back of a building, waiting for the rain to subside. Several people followed us and waited outside the shelter for us to leave that evening. He was there, the young man I worked so hard to connect with, waiting for us. One of our players gave him a Belmont jersey. He and I exchanged hugs as we prepared to leave. It was a sweet good-bye. I didn't get an opportunity to witness to him, but I know seeds of kindness and love were sown in his life that night. I leave the rest up to God, and I think of him and pray for him often.

SPONTANEITY

If there is one thing I have learned about the missions field it is to be spontaneous. You never know when you will be called on to do something, or what you will do. It was the final day of ministry in Puerto La Cruz, and we were scheduled for two more schools.

Our last stop was to be at a local school that was not in session. We had been told it would be an informal afternoon session with maybe 50 people. Initially, about 50 young people of all ages drifted in, and then the crowd turned into 100 to 150 people. Our players took turns playing groups while some of us went into the stands and interacted with the audience. We finished the afternoon with a special sharing time followed with an invitation to receive Christ. God was all over that place. I knew it was the last time I'd share the gospel on this trip to Venezuela, and I felt the power of the Holy Spirit engulf the divinely appointed time. As people prayed to receive Christ, a spirit of oneness overcame me. It was a sweet, sweet spirit in that old, dimly lighted gym, with the light of Christ illuminating the air. What a way to end our ministry!

As I walked toward the other side of the gym, a handsome young man came up to shake my hand and say thank you.

I asked him if he understood what we had just talked about, and he said he was confused. I proceeded to ask him questions, allowed him to question me, and before we finished our conversation, he said he wanted to receive Christ. We prayed together,

Betty and a new friend participate in radio interview.

and he asked Jesus into his heart. The smile on his face was priceless. When he opened his eyes, I asked him, "What did you just do?"

"I invited Jesus into my heart to be my Savior," he responded. "Thank you for talking with me and introducing me to Jesus." We hugged and I gave him a shirt, and praised God for one more convert!

And then…as we prepared to pack up and leave, a man with a radio and a telephone in his hands asked if I would be willing to be inter viewed live over the radio station. What do you think I said? "Yes, of course, I'd love to."

I answered the usual questions. Where are you from? How do you like our country? What are you doing here? How long are you staying? Then the man asked, "What message would you give to the people of Venezuela?"

Guess what I said? Yes, I shared the gospel. I told everyone listening to the broadcast that Jesus is the only hope for the world, and I told them how to have a relationship with Him. I even shared with them a prayer to pray to ask Jesus into their hearts. I thanked the Venezuelan people for receiving us and making us feel so welcomed. I ended by saying, "God bless you, and God bless Venezuela." I was speaking through a telephone receiver, and I could hear my voice, my responses to the questions, on the radio sitting on the floor next to us. What a glorious opportunity and one last chance to give a witness for Christ to only God knows how many people. Yes, a divine appointment, which highlighted for me the need to be flexible and spontaneous.

SENSITIVITY

We were in a park in the Ukraine doing street evangelism. The park was next door to a university and was a well-traveled area. We handed out tracts, witnessed, played with children, and answered questions from interested locals. I noticed an old woman, crippled, worn, bent over, walking with a cane, and carrying an old sack. She was a typical-looking, older Ukrainian woman wearing a long dress and a scarf on her head.

American youth have a special way with the elderly.

I felt drawn to her, sensitive to her torn and tattered condition.

I walked up to her and bent down to her humble frame.

"Hello, my name is Betty," I said.

She looked up at me, eye to eye, gave me a big toothless smile, and began speaking to me in her own language. I had no clue what she was saying, but I realized she was surprised, yet happy, that I had stopped her to talk. I called for a translator, and we began what would be a long and loving conversation.

She told me she was 88 years old and had survived two years in the concentration camp during the war. She lost most of her family. Basically, she was alone. I felt the need to love her and spend time with her. She had a bad sore on her leg, wrapped with a dirty cloth, and the wrinkles on her face were deep and distinctive. I told her about God's love for her and that I wanted her to know that I love her, and I wanted to pray with her. She bowed her head and I prayed.

By then the players had surrounded us to hear her story, and they joined in loving her. She smiled as several of the players had their pictures made with her, giving her wonderful hugs. It was a God-ordained moment of compassionate care for this old woman. It was difficult to leave her behind. I can still see her, turning around, looking up from her bent frame, and watching us as she walked away. I wonder where she is now and what she is doing. I think about so many people I have met along the way who needed a hug, a smile, some conversation, and sensitivity to their needs.

Caring

On one of our many drives through the countryside of Temuco, Chile, looking for opportunities to meet a need, missionary Clara Huff and I came upon an elderly Mapuche Indian woman carrying a bag of sticks on her back. It was obvious she was walking a long distance back to her home. As we slowed the car, we noticed her shoes, old and worn, with calloused and dirty feet protruding through the sides. We slowed down to pass, pulling to a stop several yards in front of her. She kept walking, not looking up as we got out of the car.

Through my local church I had collected about 50 pairs of white tennis shoes to distribute on this particular trip. Well, here was a need! We estimated her size, pulled out a pair of new shoes, and spoke to her. She stopped but did not return our greetings.

Barely looking up, she said in Spanish, "What do you want from me?" It was evident she was afraid of us.

"We don't want to hurt you. We care for you, and we have a gift for you," responded Clara as she slowly walked toward the woman. "We want you to have these shoes. God loves you, and we give you this gift in the name of His Son, Jesus." Clara handed her a Spanish tract along with the shoes.

Hesitantly, she took the shoes, nodded, and continued on her way. We got back into the car and slowly drove away.

An hour or so later, as we were driving back toward the city, we noticed in the distance someone walking down the center of the road, wearing bright-white shoes. There was the elderly woman, wearing her new tennis shoes. She moved to the side of the road when she saw the car coming. She never looked up as we met her and passed, but the shoes told the story. The mental picture of that woman and those white shoes remains vivid in my storehouse of memories. Clara and I often talk about that experience, wondering what that woman said to her family or friends when she reached her home, wearing those new, white shoes!

PATIENCE

Li Ming (not her real name) spent a year at Belmont University in the 1980s as a graduate student studying English. She came to Belmont after hearing about the university from my friend, a retired Belmont professor who was teaching in China. Li Ming was married and had one daughter, but left her family behind in Beijing while she studied here in Tennessee.

Li Ming shared stories with us about her family and the struggles they had endured while working for the communist government. Most of her time was spent working in the fields on farms, living day to day, enduring the hardships of an overbearing and overpowering social system. It was obvious she had known some very hard times.

When Li Ming came to my church, Brentwood Baptist, it was her first time to attend worship services of any kind. Each Sunday morning I made my way to Belmont and picked her up for Bible study and worship. She attended Bible study class with me and sat with friends in worship while I sang in the choir. On the way home from church Li Ming asked questions, lots of them. This was the Sunday routine for the 12 months she was in the States studying English.

I took Li Ming to other functions at the church, and she had opportunities to hear the gospel and interact weekly with people who loved and cared for her. Her questions became deeper and deeper as she searched for truth and sought to understand the gospel.

Time went by quickly, and soon her one-year stay at Belmont was coming to an end. She would be leaving in six weeks to return to China and her family.

One Sunday morning as we were driving home from church, she began asking more questions, reviewing the sermon. I knew I had to take a new approach.

"Li Ming, you are a very bright young woman. Your questions are always good, and you have learned a lot this year. You are leaving the United States in a few weeks, and I am concerned that you will go home without Jesus in your heart and life. Your head is getting in the way of your heart. Knowledge of God and His Son, Jesus, is good. Knowing Scripture is important. But, ultimately, it is a matter of the heart. That is what faith is all about—simple trust. Unless you are willing to open up your heart and let God speak to you through the Spirit, you will go back to China with a world of head knowledge, but without a relationship of faith and trust."

> "Betty, I made my connection this morning."

I continued to talk with her about the need to trust Jesus to do what He said He would do in His Word. When I left her at school and drove away, she was quiet and contemplative.

The next Sunday followed the same routine. During worship, I watched Li Ming from the choir and noticed there were times when her head was down and she wiped her eyes. I just knew God was working on her. When the service ended, we began our journey home. Before we had gone a couple of miles Li Ming said, "Betty, I made my connection this morning."

"You did what?" I responded.

"I made my connection with God today," she replied.

Then it dawned on me. "You asked Jesus into your heart?"

"Yes, I did. I opened my heart like you said I should. I trust Jesus now. I am so happy, and I feel so good."

I pulled off the highway, stopped the car, and gave her a great big hug. It was a glorious celebration of victory in a yearlong journey with Li Ming. Her joy was overflowing as we continued to talk on the way home. There were no questions this time, just pure joy! The church celebrated Li Ming's new faith in Christ Jesus with her baptism the week before she returned home to China. Li Ming is now in Beijing with her family, and she teaches English in a prominent normal school. I continue to get emails from her with photos of her family. I know that Li Ming told her family about her decision to follow Christ while in the States, but she has been careful not to push her newfound faith on anyone. I'm sure she has to be very careful in how she handles it.

Li Ming remains very special to me. I haven't seen her since her return to China some 20-plus years ago, but I still remember with much fondness the journey to help her make her "connection" with God. I think that term is so interesting, so unique to Li Ming. It took a great deal of patience to guide her and help her find that relationship with Jesus, but I would do it all over again.

LISTENING

How many lost opportunities do we have daily because we fail to listen? We can't hear because we are too busy talking. Do we answer before we know the question? Are we eager to "fix it" before we know the problem? Is the sound of silence a threat to our being? Listening seems to be a lost art these days; most of us would admit that we can be "selective" in our hearing, whether it be in our spiritual lives or in our day-to-day circumstances. We choose to hear only the parts of the message that will "fit" our plan for the moment or give us the results that meet our own personal desires.

God has taught me a lot about the art of listening through daily interruptions in my office. More and more. I am called upon to be a sounding board for students. These daily interruptions are "divine appointments" as God brings me opportunities to practice my listening skills.

I remember one day when I was consumed with a project, deep in concentration at the computer and oblivious to anything around me. I was startled back into consciousness with the thud of a backpack dropping on the floor and the sound of sobs from a broken heart. Someone was standing in front of my desk. It was Brittany, waiting for help.

I got up, walked around the desk, and closed the door. I invited her to sit down as I pulled up a chair very close to her. I simply called her name very gently and waited while the sobs continued. Finally, I said, "Tell me what has happened." Then I listened as she poured out her heart.

> Maybe, just maybe, His plans are not your plans, and His timing is not your timing.

Between sobs, Brittany said that her whole future had fallen apart. She found out from her major professor that she could not graduate at the end of the semester as anticipated, and her plans to enter graduate school to study to become a physician's assistant were going down the drain. To make a long story short, she would need to retake some courses and bring up her grades to be able to compete for admission to the graduate school of choice. Her world was tumbling down, and her dreams were shattered. She ranted and raved and yelled and screamed. Then she lashed out by saying, "God is just jerking me around."

I listened and let her get it all out, and then I said, "Brittany, first of all, this is not the end of the world. You haven't been diagnosed with cancer and given a death sentence. No one is attacking you personally. And, let's get one thing straight. God is not the one jerking you around. This is about life, and for the first time life is throwing you a curve and causing you to squirm.

"Let's talk about God and who He was last week when you were in here celebrating His love and presence and His guidance in your life. The God you stood and talked about before the church crowd two weeks ago is the same God you are accusing today of jerking you around. Maybe, just maybe, His plans are not your plans, and His timing is not your timing. You are the one who 'hurried up' your plans to graduate a semester early. You are the one who chose to come to a private school that is tough academically. You are the one who chose to be a student-athlete and try to balance academics and athletics. All those decisions have served you well, but now you are saying that it's all God's fault. Let's just take some time and think about all this."

Brittany sat in silence. Then slowly she began to look me in the eye, smile, and breath normally again. She confessed her weakness and surrendered her fears, anxieties, and frustrations to the One she proclaims as her God. She began to think rationally once again, and we proceeded to talk about what she needed to do next, a plan of action. I prayed with her and she said, "Thanks for being here for me and for listening. Now I can think clearly, and I know what I have to do."

I don't have all the answers my college students are looking for, but I know who does. God is teaching me to listen and then point them in His direction.

WILLING TO GIVE AND RECEIVE

Following a morning session in a local school, our 2009 sports evangelism team took off into the mountains outside Cape Town, South Africa, for a place called Red Hill. We drove for over an hour and a half on winding roads, narrow curves, and uneven surfaces looking for a little community where our hosts had a weekly ministry. Finally, we turned onto a very narrow pathway that was the entrance into our destination, Red Hill. And, guess what, the dirt was red! Thus, the name Red Hill.

It was one of the most impoverished places I had ever experienced—makeshift houses of old tin and scrap pieces of lumber nailed to tree trunks, held together in places by bits and pieces of scrap wire. We had stepped back in time. No cars, no phones, and electricity held in place by what looked like mangled coat hangers.

It is difficult to describe what we saw. But, once we got past the living/housing conditions, we began to see the people—the real community. Here they came to greet us! I reminded our team, "We are here for these people—let's give them all we have!"

The place was a forest of tall trees, blowing in the wind, kicking up dust and dirt and...it was cold. Our hosts dropped us off, settled us in, and told us they would return later. Had we known what "later" meant we would have kept our long pants and jackets with us. So, there we were on top of this mountain and the temperature kept dropping throughout the afternoon. The van eventually reappeared some five hours later when darkness began to overtake us.

For hours we played games (makeshift basketball and soccer) in the dust and dirt, between these shacks, amid rocks and who knows what else. They taught us their special games, we sang songs, and loved and laughed and played. It was amazing! People came out of those "tree houses," young and old, to share in the fun and activities of the afternoon.

After a couple of hours I dared to stray away from the action, absorb the environment, and walk further into the hillside community, greeting people working around their homes. "Actually, I was cold and saw some smoke and thought, there..." has to be a fire somewhere. I met an old woman, began a conversation, and she took me to a fire burning in a barrel behind her home. There I warmed my body as we talked. She invited me into her meager little house and seemed so proud to share her small space with me.

I asked her questions about her community. She said, "We feel safe here. No crime. No drugs. No one can afford them. Alcohol, yes, but no one bothers us. We are happy people. We care about our community."

I asked if I could pray for her. She smiled and responded with a big yes. She introduced me to her daughter and a sister who were in the house. I prayed for her and her family and for Red Hill. Then she walked back with me along the dirt path to the crowd, stopping along the way to greet others in their doorways. I had a powerful sense of God's presence in that place, and I also knew that it was by

His design that I was there. Later as we gave testimonies and shared the gospel I stood before those people, children and adults of all ages, and told them, "I have been all over the world, but I have never been in a more beautiful place than right here in Red Hill. This is a happy and joy-filled place. You are beautiful people, God is present here, and you have given us something special today—you have shared yourselves, your lives, and your community. We will leave a part of ourselves with you and will take with us the memory of this day spent with you."

And, you know what? The cold just became a part of the experience. We had been in a special little paradise called Red Hill. No luscious gardens or beauty as the world thinks of beauty. The beauty was in those people—their love, joy, laughter, happiness, peace, and hope. They were content with their circumstances, their community, and God's presence at this little piece of His earth. Our team came to that place to give to them, but we received so much more.

CHAPTER 4

ENDURANCE

There are numerous comparisons that could be made between the Christian life and sports. Discipline, for one, is necessary in both arenas. For the athlete, a major focus of discipline is building endurance, the ability to sustain effort over an extended period of time. The Christian too must develop endurance for the journey of life.

The writer of Hebrews captures the essence of this truth in chapter 12:1–3: "Let us run with perseverance the race marked out for us. Let us fix our eyes on Jesus, the author and perfecter of our faith, who for the joy set before him endured the cross, scorning its shame, and sat down at the right hand of the throne of God. Consider him who endured such opposition from sinful men, so that you will not grow weary and lose heart." Jesus endured the Cross by remaining focused, persevering, and never taking His eyes off the goal (joy) set before Him.

God's faithful servant, Job, was a righteous man and very rich. God allowed Satan to test Job on every side. Even though he lost everything he had and suffered from physical sickness, Job endured, never wavering in his trust in God. He was rewarded. "The LORD made him prosperous again and gave him twice as much as he had before" (Job 42:10).

Endurance is a spiritual discipline worthy of consideration. It is a part of the disciplined training that Chuck Swindoll says takes place in "the gymnasium of the soul." I like that picture!

"I AM SERVING MY JESUS"

Ewa [Eva] was the first person we met at the church where our team stayed in Poland. She and her helpers had prepared our evening meal. We soon discovered that Ewa would be cooking all our meals and caring for us during the week. She become dear to all of us and is remembered as the servant of all servants in our hearts and minds.

At first glance, she was the smiling face behind the hand that ladled soup into the bowl or served the mashed potatoes. She had the gift of hospitality. She waxed the floors, cleaned the sanctuary, and hand washed the dishes, always with a beautiful smile. Ewa was our cook, our friend, our example, smothering us with her deep sense of peace in and love for Jesus Christ.

Her story touched our hearts. Born to a Polish family in the eastern part of Poland, her mother died when she was three. Her father remarried a short time later, and Ewa gained four stepbrothers and sisters. Ewa never felt wanted in the new family. She was a part of her father's family, but she was very lonely.

She recalled World War II as a horrible time of living in fear; tragedy was constant. She told of the German and Soviet occupation of Poland, and the killing of thousands of Polish people. One night some soldiers came and took her and her family from their home, never to return. The memories of work camp, of being near starvation, and the bitterness of the winter cold are all a part of her story. As a young girl and the oldest of five children, she became the caretaker of her stepbrothers and sisters while her parents worked in the camp. Two of her brothers died in her arms as she cared for them through long, hard nights. She told of rocking one of the brothers all night to ensure he not cry and alert the soldiers, only to find that he had died in her arms during the night. Her father buried potatoes in the woods nearby so they would have enough food to survive. For two years her family lived in these conditions at a Siberian camp. By the time she was 12, her family was moved to a much "better" Russian camp. She endured the war until it ended in 1945.

> Ewa was our cook, our friend, our example.

Ewa's story is one of hope. She calls it "hope deferred." She came to know Christ personally some years following the war. Her daughter, Malvina, married Irek, the pastor of the church where we were staying. She tells her story with deep gratitude to God for allowing her to live through the war and those horrible times. She told us to expect difficult times, tests, and trials in our lives. But, she said, "God is sufficient in all things. He is your hope in every situation."

I have thought of Ewa many, many times since 1997. My interest in world history, World War II, the Holocaust, and the people who endured those times tugs at my heart frequently. I will never forget the impact of being in Poland and going to the Auschwitz-Birkenau Memorial and Museum three times with the Belmont teams. I met people whose entire families were literally destroyed.

Yes, Ewa showed us a heart of service and set the example for us to follow. From her I learned what it means to be a true, persevering servant of Christ. I remember her powerful words, "Nobody knows how many days each of us has left on this earth. I, however, know that mine are not wasted because I'm living for Jesus Christ. When I serve you these meals, I am serving my Jesus."

THE VALUE OF HARD WORK

It was a simple life for me, growing up on a farm in the small rural town of Portland, Tennessee. Everything I did revolved around three things: church, family, and school. We were a happy family: Mama, Daddy, and my older sister, Linda. Daddy was a tenant farmer. Mama kept the house and family in order and cooked a lot. We always had extra farm hands at the dinner table. After Linda and I finished elementary school,   worked outside the home, serving as the county registrar. I remember that we moved five different times; each new place had more land to tend. Linda and I were taught early in life the value of hard work as we accepted responsibilities in the home and worked on the farm. I drove the tractor, hauled hay, plowed crops with a mule, and just about anything else Daddy needed me to do. We helped milk the cows and care for the horses, goats, pigs, rabbits, baby calves, dogs, cats, chickens, and a donkey.

I loved the farm and working in the fields with my daddy. Sometimes I would be on the tractor all day by myself; breaking the ground, plowing, or whatever. That's when I would hold "church" from the seat of the tractor. I preached some good sermons, sang solos, gave an invitation, and even baptized the converts. Those fields were hallowed ground, bathed in the Spirit. It was just God and me and the tractor and those fields, preparing for a different kind of harvest.

It was a good life, simple and honorable. We respected our parents. They worked hard to provide for our needs. Discipline was expected, and we knew the value of a dollar. I remember our first television. It was black and white, and we all four pooled our money to buy it.

I found ways to earn my spending money. We all picked strawberries in the summer. I picked tomatoes for our landowner, and cut five to six lawns each week. My first public job was working at the old strawberry crate factory during strawberry season. I started with the night shift, working the belt, culling out bad berries. I would later move to a room where I used a microscope to inspect samples for disease. My next job was a Saturday job at Bentley's five-and-ten-cent store, working the candy counter for 30 cents an hour. I always saw that customers got their money's worth. After several months, I was offered a job making 40 cents an hour, working the soda fountain at Consumer's Drug Store. I became a regular there for the next four years of high school, working after school, on weekends, and during the summers. I knew everyone in town. The drug store was the gathering place for food, fellowship, gifts, and prescriptions. I made all my spending money, bought my own clothes, and didn't have to ask for money from Mama and Daddy. I learned early in life how to work hard, and I enjoyed the feeling of satisfaction at the end of each day for a job well done. Those early days and formative years provided a foundation that has served me well in life, most certainly on the missions field.

In particular, I think of my experiences in Chile during that first extended stay of living and working with missionary Clara Brincefield Huff. I got firsthand knowledge of what real commitment and missions work are all about. Our days began early, and then much of the work was done late into the evening and night when the people were most available. In fact, I watched Clara go and go, day after day, for weeks at a time and then have to come to a complete standstill from sheer exhaustion.

Overcoming Challenges

Nothing could have prepared the team of athletes for our two days of ministry in Rio das Pedras, Brazil. We worked in a favela (slum) where the "poorest of the poor" live. We were told to expect the worst living conditions we would ever see. I still remember the odor lingering in the air that just about took my breath away. Missionary Eric Reese greeted us as we stepped off the bus that first day. I had worked with Eric and his wife, Ramona, on a previous trip to Rio, and it was great to see them again.

They live and work in Rio das Pedras, and they classify the 90,000 people in this area into three categories: the working poor who live in small terra-cotta-black homes; the poor who live in the wooden shacks that surround the working poor; and the desperately poor who live on the street or in flimsy, temporary structures on the perimeter of town. Utilities are a mix of home-remedy connections that sometimes include coat hangers as part of electrical tie-ins. Municipal water is scarce and unevenly distributed within the community. The street is a combination of muddy path, open sewer, and marginally covered sewage trench. Many of the streets in the favela are not much wider than an American's outstretched arms. Images on television or video do not adequately describe the living conditions, the smell, and the near claustrophobic closeness of the spaces in Rio das Pedras.

According to Eric, the good news is that the drug cartels, so prevalent in the majority of favelas, have been kept at bay, and the crime rate is very low in the area. For those who live here, there is no distinction in class, color, ethnic origin, or social status—they are all in the same boat and doing their best to survive. From what we witnessed, even the crudest of homes are clean and neat, yet sparsely furnished. The children are clothed and as clean as possible.

There is no way to estimate the number of children who showed up in the town square for our first of two days of ministry. They were everywhere and looked like an organizer's worst nightmare; yet, they were responsive to our directions as we prepared for drills and play. No one complained that the sun was scorching or that the little paved area was even hotter. Six hours of sweat and bug bites did nothing to dampen our spirits. We decided not to drink from the bottles of water that we had brought with us. The children had nothing to drink, and it didn't seem fair for us to drink in front of them. I prayed our team members would not succumb to dehydration.

Our last day was a day of play, sharing the gospel, and witnessing with the kids we had met the day before. Many of the kids responded to the call to receive Christ, just as they had daily throughout the week. Then the challenge came from the older youth to play a soccer game against the local club team. We were not soccer players but the team responded, "Yes, we will play."

> I prayed our team members would not succumb to dehydration.

Anyone watching would never have known that we had been on our feet for six days and nights. Whatever the request, our team responded to the challenge. Our team "left it all on the court," meaning they were totally spent for Christ! We had overcome in His strength.

A challenge of a different kind met me and a team from my local church, Brentwood Baptist, when we did a sports camp in Dundee, Scotland. We worked with five churches in Dundee, conducting sports camps during the day and working with street kids at night. The night sessions were the challenge. The teenagers showed up dressed in clothes representative of the gangs in the city. Black jackets, black jeans, black shoes, black T-shirts, and dyed hair, mostly black. They had gold chains, earrings, bandanas, and attitudes. They cursed; they strutted; and they tested our patience. They came to the church out of curiosity and the need to make a statement. And, make a statement they did. We were told to watch our backs and to be careful after dark. The church had experienced broken windows from beer bottles thrown by some of these same youth. We had a variety of activities planned from arts and crafts, to cooking, and country/line dancing. Our quiet time for Bible study, testimonies, and sharing the gospel stretched our limits. It was a challenge just to organize and keep their attention.

I was in a small group of teenagers. We gave each one a Bible to use for the evening. I watched one young girl rip a page from the Bible we had given her. My heart broke. I could not believe what I was seeing. I became angry and told her how precious the words on that page were. It was important that we take a stand. We threatened to send them away if they didn't cooperate. They did not want to leave, so we knew God had brought them there for a purpose. Some would ask questions just to act smart and get attention. There were times when I felt absolutely useless, unable to communicate with youth for the first time in my life. We all felt defeated.

One particular night, our team met afterwards to process the events of the evening. We confessed our limitations, our frustrations, and our lack of control. We wept, and we prayed. We acknowledged before God and one another that these kids were beyond our control. We recognized that if anything good came from our efforts that week it would have to come from God. We relinquished control and gave it all to Him.

Night after night they came. Little by little, they warmed up to us. They listened more and more, and were less disruptive and more attentive. They began to ask legitimate questions. They became curious about this God we served and about this Jesus who could be their friend. They finally responded to our physical touch without becoming defensive. Some even accepted our hugs and returned them. We praised God for these victories. The adults from the churches began to embrace the kids that they had once feared. Some came to worship on Sunday, the first time they had ever been in a church worship service.

Meeting the challenge of connecting with those gang members taught me a lot during that trip. It is not by our own strength but through the power of God's Word and the Holy Spirit that barriers can be broken down and hearts softened. There are no walls too great or rivers too wide that God cannot cross. "For our struggle is not against flesh and blood, but against the rulers, against the authorities, against the powers of this dark world and against the spiritual forces of evil.... Therefore put on the full armor of God, so that when the day of evil comes, you may be able to stand your ground" (Ephesians 6:12–13). I also claim the verse that says, "not by might and not by power, but by my Spirit says the LORD" (Zechariah 4:6).

HUNGRY, IF ONLY FOR THE NIGHT

In May 1995, I agreed to lead my first sports evangelism missions team from Belmont to Poland, a northern European country slightly smaller than New Mexico, with a population close to 40 million. We were housed at the partially renovated Baptist seminary at Rahdosk, outside the city limits of Warsaw.

Our drive from the airport to the seminary was an adventure, with long-legged basketball players packed into a minivan and a couple of minicars. The last mile took nearly an hour and was on a dirt road filled with potholes unlike any ruts I had ever seen. We soon learned that those rides were few and far between. They were replaced by a mile walk to catch a train, followed by a 45-minute ride to Warsaw, ending with a 20-minute walk to a school for our ministry. Our days were long, beginning with the walk at 7:00 A.M. and ending some days as late as 10:00 P.M. And, the same one-mile walk in the early morning through the woods to catch the train had to be retraced at night, in the dark. Now when it is dark in the Polish countryside, it is seriously dark! We were carrying bags of basketballs, tennis shoes, personal items, and one flashlight.

We had our breakfast at the seminary. That consisted of warm powdered milk, with a few noodles swimming around, bread, butter, and hot tea. Our first evening meal was cheese, bread, sliced cucumbers, and hot tea. The players did take advantage of our noon treks to McDonald's in downtown Warsaw and to a small fried chicken place we discovered by accident. We had taken light snacks in our bags, thinking we might need some extras at night, but those snacks were gone after the first two days. Remember we were burning tons of calories each day in the sports camps.

After a couple of days of this schedule, two of our male basketball players, Kerry West and Kevin Fields, knocked at my door about 11:00 P.M.

"B-Dub [as in W]," Kerry said. "We're hungry. We can't sleep. Do you have any food?"

"No," I responded. "You've already exhausted my supply. Just go to bed, close your eyes, and go to sleep. That's all I know to do."

The two athletes just stood there, unable to speak. It was a new experience for them, going to bed hungry. We would laugh about that night for years to come. All of us lost weight on that trip. However, we all learned a valuable lesson and gained an understanding, even if slight, into the plight of millions around the world who go to bed hungry every night.

Today, when I visit with Kevin and his wife, Tiffany, and their two daughters, Carragan and Kaylea Wiseman, our conversation always includes the memory of that night in Poland. Kevin says he and Tiffany will be lying in bed at night, ready for sleep, and one of them will say, "I'm hungry." The other will answer, "Just close your eyes and go to sleep. That's all I know to do."

Kevin and Kerry were high school and college basketball teammates and remain dear friends and brothers in Christ today. They were with me on that initial trip to Poland and returned to the country with me the next two years for ministry. Then they accompanied me the following year to Costa Rica as Belmont began three years of ministry in that country. Kerry is now married to his college sweetheart, Courtney, and they have a baby girl named Kaylor.

The men marvel at how God has worked in their lives to take them all over the world together, allowing them to use their God-given basketball talents to share the good news of Jesus Christ.

And, they will never forget discovering what it means to be hungry!

SURPRISE! THE HEAT IS FOR REAL!

Our team arrived in Caracas, Venezuela, on schedule. As we transitioned through customs and made our way, with lots of luggage, to another terminal for the next leg of our journey, we got our first introduction to the heat we were told to expect. It hit us boldly in the face. Yes, it was seriously hot and difficult to breathe. We all began to perspire from the extreme heat, and the long walk with luggage was a struggle. I thought, How in the world will we withstand this heat for ten days?

The team endured soaring temperatures in Venezuela.

The days ahead were packed with ministry, and the sun was hot! I remember on one particular day we were all so hot and sweaty from spending the morning in the sun, and then we were escorted into a small, dimly lighted classroom. There we were served rice and beans, bottled soda, and water (with no ice) for lunch. It was hot food in a stuffy room after a hot morning in the sun. Then it was back onto the burning concrete court under the 115-degree heat (yes, 115 degrees) for the afternoon. *"Lord, send us some clouds, please"* was my prayer. I don't believe I have ever been as hot as I was that day. But, you know what, God did send us some clouds off and on throughout the afternoon, and we were blessed with some protection from the scorching heat.

My fair skin took a beating in the Venezuelan sun during that trip. There was no way to protect against it—even sunscreen was not effective. I prayed a lot, *"God, protect us."* Of course, for the young college students, the sun was just what they needed to enhance their dark tans. However, they too, were challenged by the extreme heat.

> "He will satisfy your needs in a sun-scorched land."

And it wasn't just our team that struggled. We were sitting at a local restaurant one evening having a late dinner following a long day of sun-soaked ministry. I noticed our missionary host looked tired, and he was somewhat quiet. He said he had a splitting headache. Finally, he said, "I hope I can keep up with you guys. I never expected the energy required to do what you all do all day long, day after day. It is only the second day of ministry, and I'm beat. I'm not used to this. My head is hurting, my body is sore, and I am worn out. But, I will recover and be ready tomorrow." Yes, he recovered, and he was ready the next day. This was his first experience with the demands of sports evangelism.

Each morning prior to leaving for the day's ministry, I shared with the team Scripture verses that I had claimed for that particular day. One that seemed appropriate was Isaiah 58:11: "The LORD will guide you always; He will satisfy your needs in a sun-scorched land and will strengthen your frame. You will be like a well-watered garden, like a spring whose waters never fail." It was only by God's favor that we were able to endure and continue our missions work.

ALL KINDS OF ENERGY

I was preparing a team of basketball players for the May 2008 trip back to Rio de Janeiro, Brazil. About 15 years earlier, I began leading sports evangelism missions trips yearly, and sometimes twice yearly. The previous year I began to feel my body age a little; I knew I was slowing down in many ways, becoming less active. I had turned 65 in February and had received tons of communications from the social security office regarding retirement and a lot of other junk mail relating to my age. My mind began playing tricks on my body by sending messages that I was getting too old to do sports evangelism and the physically challenging duties of leading such trips. Also, I was seeing some physical changes in my body that result from aging. The devil got in my head, and I began to question myself, Can I still do this? I began thinking that maybe I was getting too old to be effective in this kind of ministry.

Leading a sports team requires energy—physical, mental, emotional, and spiritual energy. It consumes a person's resources. The focus required is daunting. A leader must set the tone and pace for everyone else. Time is of the essence and cannot be wasted. A schedule must be followed, getting from place to place, and on someone else's time frame. It requires discipline, punctuality, flexibility, commitment, thinking ahead, and taking the lead. Walking onto a basketball court or into a sporting facility, taking charge and organizing anywhere from 200 to 800 kids of all ages for play, demands resources that can only come from years of experience in teaching and coaching. The connection with people is instantaneous and the ministry begins when one gets off the bus and sees the very first person. First impressions are lasting impressions. What they see is what they get!

Connecting with a crowd is the key if you want to have their attention when it comes time to share the gospel. You must earn your audience. I jump, skip, run, clap, and lead cheers; dribble and shoot the ball; work the crowd by organizing the wave, rah-rah, and high-fives. I also lead groups of kindergarteners who have come in to watch in a game of "duck, duck, goose" or pretending to be a train; making small circles with small balls; and on and on. I do whatever is needed to keep them active and engaged. The little girl inside of me loves to come out and play.

On the other hand, I must keep my team pumped and energized, recognizing when there is a lull and meeting the challenge of inspiring them. All the time, I am sizing up the crowd and thinking ahead about how we'll get them organized, quiet, and attentive to listen to the message we will leave with them. It is a constant thought process, along with physical demands. Then I must be totally focused emotionally and spiritually for God to speak through me as I share the gospel and follow the leading of the Holy Spirit in how and when to give an invitation to a crowd. I never try to just "wing it" or "fly by the seat of my pants." My task requires that I be in tune with God, focused on what He has orchestrated, and be flexible enough to be used by Him. There are times that we do all this three times a day and in three different settings. Then, I must try to get rest at night. There is little time for playing around when I get back to the hotel or place of residence.

I prayed a lot prior to this particular trip in 2008, for God to restore me to full physical capacity and prepare me for the demands of the work. And, He did! I can honestly say that when I walked into the airport to meet my team and check in for the long overnight flight

Connecting with a crowd is important.

it all came back to me. I thought, this is just adrenaline. It won't last. But, it did last! I was reenergized unlike I had been in years. I felt better than I had in months. That's what passion for ministry does to you. That is what being "on mission" does for you. Call it a high or whatever, but I know that I am at my very best when I am serving my God. Age is one thing, but the state of the heart is the driving force.

> I know that I am at my very best when I am serving my God.

It is a God-thing. Can I do this on my own? No. Am I capable of continuing these yearly demands? Yes, I know "I can do everything through him who gives me strength" (Philippians 4:13). When God calls us, He provides for all our needs. I realize retirement from the university and my work is inevitable, and if God wants me to continue to do missions trips, He will not only provide the financial and other resources as He always has, but also, I am confident He will provide all the physical resources for the demands of this ministry.

I remember a mother who had come to a clinic with her child and, following the two-hour session, prayed with me to receive Christ. During our conversation, she said to me, "You have so much energy. I love your enthusiasm and excitement for what you do."

I replied, "Thank you. But, it isn't me. God is the source of all my energy," as I put my hand to my heart and pointed upward!

REQUIRED FOCUS

I discovered a new and different level of focus and intensity in sharing the gospel when I participated in two medical missions trips to Rio, Brazil, sponsored by my local church. The team of around 40 people was made up of doctors, nurses, pharmacists, dentists, eye-care professionals, and several volunteers. Four of us had volunteered to do evangelism.

Although different from my sports evangelism missions trips, these trips were experiences of a lifetime for me. First, I was not the leader. I was a follower and not in charge. I do enjoy just serving and following. I always try to be an encourager to the leader because I know how much work is required.

The first day of a medical missions trip is always a humbling experience. People are everywhere—lines upon lines of men, women, children—waiting for an opportunity to see the doctors. Most of them have been in line all night.

Each of the four of us who did evangelism was placed in four strategic places, sometimes with the lines and sometimes in a small room with eight to ten chairs. We each were assigned a translator who stayed with us all day long. That little room became a sanctuary where revival was experienced all day long for five days. Each person who came for medical attention was brought to one of us for spiritual counseling. The first day I spent all day in a medical clinic sharing the gospel was unlike anything else I had ever experienced.

Imagine this scenario. A small group of people is ushered in and the door is closed. With my Bible in hand and speaking through a translator, I begin by saying something like: "I know you have come to see the doctor and get medical care today. While you are waiting in line, I want to share something very important with you. Everything I will share with you today is from God's Word, the Bible. This is God's word for all people of the world."

The focus and the intensity level of those moments was a powerful testimony of how God works. The little room became church.

I proceeded to share the gospel, adapting to the situation, using the simple outline noted in chapter 1 of this book. I talked about how to have a relationship with Jesus Christ and how important that is in one's life. I told them that each of us who traveled from the United States has this relationship. They listened intently as I took them through the plan of salvation. When I asked if they wanted to receive Christ, I was overwhelmed at the response. When someone said, "I am a believer," I asked them to join me in praying for the others. The room reverberated with the sound of people praying to receive Christ.

Betty shared the plan of salvation with people waiting to see a doctor in Rio, Brazil.

There were lots of children. If the children were old enough to understand, I asked them to sit on the floor in front of their parents and listen. I usually had an extra volunteer in the room to help with small children. Sometimes babies were in the room, and I was attentive to mothers caring for these babies. It was not uncommon for a mother to nurse her baby as we shared the gospel. I remember one woman who had a baby on each breast and a small child leaning on her lap. I did not miss a beat. She listened and later prayed to receive Christ.

A woman came into the room with a daughter who looked to be around ten years old. Following the presentation of the gospel, I went from person to person and asked, "Do you want to ask Jesus into your heart?"

This particular woman said no, and I proceeded to ask her daughter. "Do you understand what I have been saying?"

She nodded yes.

I said, "Do you want to invite Jesus into your heart?"

"Yes, I do," she responded.

Her mother was a little taken aback. She said something to her daughter in Portuguese, and her daughter told her she wanted to make this decision. I talked to the mother through the translator and told her this was a personal decision that must be made individually.

Finally, I said, "Your daughter wants this personal relationship. This is the most important decision she will ever make. Don't you want to reconsider and join her in making your own decision, along with her?"

She looked at her daughter, took her hand, and smiled at her, and then a big tear rolled down her cheek. She turned to me with an even bigger smile and said, "I want to make the decision too."

They prayed together, mother and daughter, to receive Christ that day. When we finished praying the mother stood and ran up to me; she gave me a big hug and thank you.

"Thank you," she said, "for introducing us to Jesus, and for not giving up on me."

Another woman who prayed that same day was overwhelmed. She hugged me and said, "Thank you for introducing me to Jesus. Now I understand. I've been waiting all my life for someone to explain all this to me. Thank you, thank you!"

All day long, day after day, story after story, I shared Jesus and invited people into a relationship with Him. What a glorious and humbling opportunity! But, it required a focus and intensity level unlike any other experience.

At the end of each day, we delivered commitment cards to the team leader with names, addresses, and decisions that were made so that the pastor of the local church could follow-up. We praised God for new converts and the difference the experiences of the days made in our own lives. It was a weeklong revival.

On the Sunday before we left for the trip to Rio, my pastor, Mike Glenn, preached from Jeremiah 8:20–22: "The harvest is past, the summer has ended, and we are not saved. Since my people are crushed, I am crushed; I mourn, and horror grips me. Is there no balm in Gilead? Is there no physician there? Why then is there no healing for the wound of my people?" Jeremiah, known as the "weeping prophet," was crying out on behalf of his people. There was a sense of urgency in Jeremiah's cry!

I felt God asking me: *Betty, do you have this kind of urgency for the people I am sending you to? Are you willing to weep on their behalf?*

I claimed Jeremiah 8:20–22 for that trip. I have not forgotten that sermon and my affinity to Jeremiah and his love for his people.

CHAPTER 5

PREPARATION

F or I know the plans I have for you,' declares the LORD, 'plans to prosper you and not to harm you, plans to give you hope and a future'" (Jeremiah 29:11). What a great promise! This verse tells us all we need to know about preparation for all that is ahead of us. For me, the greatest joy of growing older in my faith is looking back on my life and seeing how God really did have a plan for my life. I can see where things that happened through the years—things I could not understand at the time—were just a part of the process of preparation for all He had in store for me.

I tell my students that the prize is in the process. God, through all our experiences in life, is readying us for His bigger purpose and plan. The longer we are on the anvil, the more prepared we will ultimately become.

ELVIRA

It was the summer before my senior year in high school. Elvira, a missionary to migrants, came to my hometown, Portland, Tennessee, to work with the Mexicans who had settled in for a summer of picking strawberries and harvesting tobacco crops. Migrant workers were annual visitors to our rural town during the summer months. Their living conditions—barns, makeshift shelters, and condemned houses—moved me to tears.

I volunteered through my church to drive Elvira to the various campsites on Sunday nights to lead Bible study and worship for the migrant workers. Our association of churches provided an old station wagon for her, but she did not have a driver's license. I was her shadow on Sunday afternoons and evenings throughout the summer. Or maybe she was my shadow—Elvira stood 5-feet-1-inch tall and I was 5-feet-11-inches.

Elvira spoke Spanish and was a dynamite communicator of the gospel. When she spoke, the people listened. My responsibility, other than driving her to the people, was to organize the children for play and recreation while she worked with the adults and shared the good news of Jesus Christ. I loved and hugged on the children and we played games, but all the while I was watching Elvira share Christ with great enthusiasm. I admired her work and love for these people, and I envied her ability to speak Spanish and communicate. I longed to talk to the people, but I had to settle for communication with my heart.

Because of that experience, I chose to take Spanish classes in college. I can look back now and see that experience was one of many through the years in my preparation for my passion for and involvement in missions.

PREPARING IN THE WILDERNESS

Just prior to my missions experience in Chile in 1992, I had been through what I now call my wilderness experience. Heartache had consumed me. In 1986, my mother was diagnosed with acute leukemia. I was with her at the oncologist's office when he said, "You have six weeks to live." My world began to crumble right before my eyes. We were told that extensive chemotherapy might extend her life, but we could not be sure how long.

Mom died ten months later at Baptist Hospital in Nashville. During that time, I was consumed with helping Mom and Dad. She spent three of those last eight months in the hospital getting chemotherapy. I taught classes, did my work at school, and got to the hospital by 6:00 P.M. to spend the night with Mom and Dad. Daddy cared for her during the day, and had a bed in her room so he could sleep during the nights. I slept on a cot and got up and down with her during the night. When she was in remission and at home, I went home each weekend to clean, cook, and care for my parents. Mom died on May 23, 1987. I lost my best friend, and the adjustment was a yearlong process. I continued to run back and

> My world began to crumble right before my eyes.

forth, an hour's drive one way, to the farm in Portland to care for my dad.

Dad was lonely, and eventually met a very young woman with three small children. She was younger than me! A year later, they were married. This was a tumultuous time in the life of our family. The age difference was difficult to accept and my sister and I fought it; but, finally, we concluded that it was Dad's life, and we were not in control. The marriage created a lot of friction and much heartache early on for all of us. It is the only time in my life I can remember being at odds with my dad.

However, I was determined to keep a good relationship with my dad. I remember a sermon on forgiveness by my former pastor, Pastor Wilson. I responded during the invitation by walking the aisle and telling Brother Wilson I needed help with forgiveness. He knew my circumstances, and he prayed with me to let go. When the service concluded I drove straight to my dad's

> For the first time in my life I understood the peace that comes from forgiving someone.

house and asked him to forgive me for anything I had said or done to hurt him. I told him I forgave him for the hurt he had caused in my life. He didn't understand all that meant on that particular day, but it was the beginning of some healing for me. And, it opened our relationship back up for fellowship. For the first time in my life I understood the peace that comes from forgiving someone. Dad and his wife, Christel, were happily married for almost 20 years when he died on October 28, 2009, just five weeks shy of his 95th birthday. I loved him as much as a daughter could love a father, and I know he loved me and was proud of me.

Again, just before that first overseas missions trip in 1992, my brother-in-law, Shag McCown, was diagnosed with a rare form of cancer. My sister, Linda, a diabetic, was bitten by a brown recluse spider, resulting in the amputation of her right leg. I spent a year or so consumed with caring for Linda and Shag. The loss of Linda's leg was like a death for me. It took me years to accept this part of her being gone. I was their principal caregiver, and I was committed to the task.

Linda and I cared for Shag at home as long as we could before admitting him to a nursing home. For Linda, the trauma of that experience was devastating, but she amazed us all with her courage and determination to continue her role as a teacher at the local high school in Lebanon. With her new prosthesis and crutches, Linda continued to teach, and she visited her beloved Shag daily at the nursing home until he died a year later.

I had taken on the burdens of my family in these tragic circumstances. I look back now and see how trapped I had allowed myself to become. I suppressed so much hurt and pain. My personal way of dealing with these things was to take control and work, work, work. It became a pattern in my life, trying to control and fix things. I had no other life except my teaching and caring for family. I didn't have time for church, and I could not see God in any of this. I couldn't even pray.

It is very painful to write about this particular part of my life's journey. Where had all the joy in my life gone? I could not remember what the sound of my own laughter was like. It was a wilderness experience for me. I needed to be freed from the depths of despair.

I started teaching stress management classes at school, and I learned a lot from researching to teach the class. I learned that people have a need to control. I discovered I was a control freak. Yet, I could not fix my family situations, nor could I control the circumstances. I just needed to let go. It took a while, but I finally let go of a lot of things, and I let God take control of my life unlike I ever had. As I look back, I can see God's provision and faithfulness to me. Everything I had been through was part of His plan and had a purpose. It was a necessary part of the preparation for the rest of my life, and all He had in store for me.

It was about this time that I said yes to my first overseas missions trip to Chile. It was a life-changing trip—part of my freeing up. I learned a lot from my wilderness experience. I learned that *"Wow, God! You were in control all along, and I just could not let go."* God used my wilderness experience to get me ready, to prepare me, for a new passion and purpose in life.

Sufficiency

We arrived in San Jose, Costa Rica, in the early afternoon and settled in our quarters around 3:30 P.M. "Can you be ready to go at 4:30? You are scheduled to give a clinic at 6:00 P.M. Hope you don't mind that we have you heavily scheduled," said our missionary hostess.

Of course we would be ready. God prepared the way. High schools, middle schools, elementary schools, a technological institute, sport clubs—doors were open—morning, evening, and night. We talked about drugs, alcohol, making choices. Tell us why you are here. What does the cross around your neck mean to you? Why is Jesus so important to you? A personal relationship—how do you get it? WWJD—what would Jesus do? What is that? They asked questions; they heard personal testimonies of Christ's presence in our lives; they listened; and they wanted to talk. It didn't take long to see why we were in Costa Rica. God had put us there—it was His trip.

Whatever the conditions, God prepared the way.

We soon forgot about wooden basketball courts. Concrete greeted us, sometimes just an asphalt driveway—no gym, no court. We experienced hot sunshine and sweat, mosquitoes and ants, and consumed lots of bottled water. We played, taught, gave demonstrations, shared, laughed, cried, and worked. And we witnessed to hundreds of young people and adults. If they came to see basketball, they didn't get away without hearing about Christ. We certainly were out of our comfort zone, but God was in control and that was all that mattered.

Sunday afternoon we were outside an old gymnasium with the local pastor and many of the local youth, waiting for the doors to open. I received a telephone call from Nashville. My friend and colleague and department chair at Belmont, Bill Bandy, had died from a massive heart attack the day before. It just could not be! The healthiest man in the world; but, it was true. I was in total shock! I fell apart! We all crumbled!

But it didn't take long for God to reveal Himself and His powerful touch. We chose to finish what He had begun in us, to depend on God's goodness and mercy, and to claim Psalm 121: "I will lift up my eyes unto the hills—where does my help come from? My help comes from the LORD, the Maker of heaven and earth."

> I was in total shock! I fell apart! We all crumbled!

Never has that Scripture been more meaningful to me. God moved in a mighty way that night as our players gave testimonies in worship before the gathered crowd. The local pastor told the audience about our tragic loss, and he explained how he had seen God at work in our team's lives. I don't believe I've ever experienced the amount and range of emotions in one day as we did that Sunday. Late that night, back at the hotel, we continued to process the events of the day and God's work in us. We truly experienced God in an awesome way. All of us will treasure the day and all that happened, even in the face of death and despair, far away from home.

I was reminded of how missionaries all over the world face the deaths of family and friends in faraway places on a regular basis. What a sacrifice, one of so many, they make. I felt oneness of spirit with these brothers and sisters in Christ who struggle with things that we Christians at home take for granted, the freedom to grieve with those we love when processing pain and death. God is sufficient in all circumstances to meet our needs.

FLEXIBILITY

In May 2001, on a return trip to Portugal, God taught us a lot about flexibility. We had moved from town to town, spending two to three days ministering in each place. We left immediately following the Sunday services in the town of Abrantes to travel three hours to Moura where we were to finish our ministry. We stopped in Évora to see the ruins of an ancient Roman temple, cathedrals, megalithic monuments, and other sites. The countryside was a welcomed reprieve after living in the outskirts of the big city of Lisbon. The cork trees and olive vineyards presented a different backdrop of Portugal.

Upon arrival and checking in at the local hotel a very dark cloud appeared, bringing thunder, lightning, and torrents of rain. Streets were flooded and impassable. Our host missionary, Sharon Ford, was caught in the flooding as she attempted to return to Lisbon after dropping us off. Her car died, and she was forced to stay in Moura. This presented lots of frustration for her and her husband, Steve. They had not made plans for both of them to be away from home. Sharon had no bag; thus, no clothes. However, we would know of God's hand in this on Tuesday.

Tuesday was totally and completely God-planned, God-filled, and God-inspired. We were outside on asphalt courts, protected from the potentially dangerous hot sun by cloudy skies. The day was filled with opportunities for witnessing and sharing the gospel. Sharon came to know why the storm had kept her from returning. She witnessed continuously. Steve recognized immediately that he could not have handled the translation by himself. Local students gave Sharon and Steve their names and phone numbers. They wanted to know about this Jesus. Why has no one told us before? Tell us more! There was only one church in the town, a Catholic church, and it was closed. We discovered it is an empty region without a religion of any kind, but with a God who waits for them to hear and respond.

At the end of the day, Sharon's tears kept coming. She was trying to process what all this meant. There was absolute joy! She said, "I witnessed more and had more people ask me about Jesus in one day than I have had in eight years of missionary work in Portugal. Now I know why the storm and rain washed away my plans. God needed me here."

Several girls were at the hotel the next morning to see Sharon as we checked out. She and Steve planned a return visit in two weeks to help with follow-up and to reach out to some young girls who were eager to know more. I am convinced the experience was just a beginning of a more concentrated effort to spread the gospel in this town.

The local radio station and newspaper invited a pastor friend, Steve, and me to come for an interview in the late afternoon. I took two of my Belmont athletes with us. They had made pictures of our ministry earlier in the day for the newspaper. We had a 30-minute live interview about our visit and our purpose for coming. We openly shared the gospel on the radio, and only God knows where those seeds fell.

I am convinced that God is in control of circumstances that arise in our lives, just like He used that storm to ensure that some young people in Moura heard about Jesus. God turned frustration into joy as His will unfolded and we were forced to be flexible. It was the climax of a God-inspired, God-filled time of ministry in Portugal.

God answered the prayer we claimed for the week, the prayer of Jabez. God blessed us and our ministry for His glory. God's hand was upon us and our efforts. So much of what happened cannot be explained any other way. God expanded our territory and our opportunities. He expanded the territory of missionaries Steve and

Sharon Ford. And, God kept us from harm, kept us safe, and free from pain. We experienced changes in weather, climate, and time. Travel is always a concern. Physical energy is especially demanding for this kind of ministry. Just as God granted Jabez his request in 1 Chronicles, God granted our request and answered our prayer!

GIFTED AND EQUIPPED

The first time I met Brandon Owen, he had just graduated from high school and was working as a student instructor at one of our men's summer basketball camps. I had just returned from a sports evangelism missions trip to Costa Rica. As I stood watching the campers, a member of the team from the trip to Costa Rica brought Brandon to the doorway of the gym to meet me.

"B-Dub, this is Brandon Owen; he will be a freshman here this fall. I have been sharing about our missions trip to Costa Rica, and he is a good candidate for future trips."

In conversation with Brandon that morning, I discovered his mother, Cindy, was one of my former students, and his father, Bill, was a pastor at Mt. Carmel Baptist Church in Cross Plains, Tennessee. Brandon and I became immediate friends, and over the next six years, while he did his undergraduate and graduate work at Belmont, we shared four missions trips together. I was moved, from the beginning, by his love for Jesus and his energy, enthusiasm, and desire to share this love with others.

> Brandon was dynamite on the missions field. His smile was a light in any circumstance.

Brandon was a member of missions teams that worked in Portugal for two consecutive years and in Rio, Brazil, in May 2002, his senior year. He returned to Rio with me following completion of his graduate studies in May 2004. What I observed in Brandon during those six years is a story worth sharing.

Brandon grew up in a wonderful Christian home, attended a Baptist church, and was consistently involved in Bible study, choir, and youth activities. His life revolved around his home, the church, and his God-given talents as a high school athlete. His two younger brothers, both athletes, completed the "all-American family."

Brandon was grounded in his faith and confident in his salvation. We spent precious time together in my office during those first few years as he shared his burden for his lost friends. Our conversations almost always led to a prayertime where we prayed for those friends by name. And, I remember how Brandon agonized over Christian friends he claimed would not "walk the walk or talk the talk."

Many times I reminded Brandon that the majority of these student friends had not grown up in the church and "cut their teeth" on the gospel. I think he had the idea that because they professed Christ that they should all be as mature in their faith as he was. Many times I prayed with Brandon that God would give him patience as he waited on God to do a work in their lives. He needed to see that their journey was different from his. I thought this should be the focal point of his walk as a Christian friend. Brandon was always receptive to advice, leadership, and growth.

Brandon was dynamite on the missions field. His contagious spirit, energy, and spontaneous engagement of the people were a joy to behold. His smile was a light in any circumstance. I watched him run, jump, and play with kids. I saw him capture the attention of young people in small groups as he shared his faith. He hugged and loved and invited people into God's kingdom.

What interested me the most about Brandon's journey in missions was his transition from sharing the gospel to guiding someone into a personal relationship with Christ. He was always good at witnessing and walking through the plan of salvation. Then I saw him move to another level of witnessing; carrying that plan into a how-to and actually leading someone to receive Christ.

His last trip with me to Brazil was life changing. Over and over, he experienced God's divine appointments with people who listened to his witness and prayed to receive Christ. His cup was filled and running over with excitement as he allowed God to use him as a living vessel of the Great Commission. Only God knows the seeds he planted and the number of converts for which he was responsible. It thrilled my soul to see Brandon evolve into a true disciple of Jesus Christ.

And, this journey continues. Brandon is a high school teacher and coach. He and his wife, Leslie Ann, both work with the youth of their church and now lead yearly youth missions trips.

PERSONAL TESTIMONY

Now I want to get into some practical steps to preparation for a missions trip. It is important that we always be prepared to give a short three-minute personal testimony of who Christ is in our life and the difference a relationship with Him makes. I encourage all our team members, once they have been selected and we begin meeting, to write out their testimony. This causes them to reflect, think through, and put in concise words what they would say if called upon to give a testimony. For someone who has never shared a testimony, it is a good way to begin working toward that goal.

Below is my very first written testimony required for an Evangelism Explosion class I took at my church 30 years ago. I have saved it all these years, because it served as a starting point for me in writing and sharing my testimony. I share it with you as an example to encourage you.

Hello, my name is Betty Wiseman from Nashville, Tennessee, in the United States. I am a professor of Health & Physical Education at Belmont University, a Baptist university in Nashville. I am a Christian, and I have come to your country to share with you my friend, Jesus Christ, and His love for you.

I grew up on a farm and was fortunate as a child to

have been brought up in a Christian home where my parents took me to church regularly. It was the thing to do around our house and a vital part of our family life. At age 11, I asked Jesus into my heart, accepting His promise of eternal life—not fully understanding what all that meant, but knowing I was trusting Christ to do what He said He would do.

Upon receiving this gift of eternal life and a personal relationship with Christ, many changes began to take place in my life. I felt a real joy and a sense of security I had not known before, and those same feelings grow stronger even today. My life took on new direction and meaning as Jesus became Lord of my life.

Jesus Christ's presence in my life is a source of strength and comfort as I face each new day. Through daily Bible study and prayer He becomes more real and personal in my everyday walk as a Christian. He has blessed me abundantly with good Christian friends and fellowship through the ministry of my church. But, you know, there are times in my life when I am afraid; I get lonely and sad; I hurt; I get discouraged; I feel defeated; and I sin. But I thank God that He is always faithful and replaces these feelings with peace, joy, happiness, forgiveness, and love.

The Bible says "God is love"—I have found this to be my greatest source of strength. I know God loves me and cares for me and He is my friend—He meets all my needs. He can look beyond all my weaknesses, my faults. The Bible teaches that anyone who will confess his sin and trust Jesus can find that same forgiveness, peace, and happiness that I found.

I enjoy people, I have a zest for and a love for life—but I guess I am like most people—I don't like the thought of dying. Yet, I have a peace and assurance, which comes through my relationship with Jesus Christ, that death is not the end but will bring for me eternal life. I know that when I die I will go to heaven to live with Him forever. You can have that same assurance of eternal life by asking Jesus into your heart. That is my prayer for you today.

PRAYER

Prayer is foundational in the preparation for any evangelism endeavor. Show me evidence of one's personal prayer life, and I will predict the impact of that person's ministry. I would not think about putting a team together without first bathing the opportunity and prospects in prayer. I am only the instrument for creating a team, not the one who is making the call. Much thought and prayer go into the selection of team members.

Once the team is confirmed, a new level of prayer begins for me personally. I know my team members and their gifts and abilities. I pray for each one regularly as God prepares their heart for the upcoming ministry. We have team meetings for three months prior to the trip to plan, encourage, motivate, and pray. I find these student-athletes relish the meetings as a time to draw away from daily demands of school and athletics and focus for a short time on the call that they have accepted.

> Much thought and prayer go into the selection of team members. I pray for each one regularly.

Each team member is encouraged to enlist prayer partners from family, church, and friends who will join our team as prayer warriors throughout the preparations and during the actual on-the-field ministry. The prayer partners receive an invitation to send prayer grams via the online journal once it is in place.

Most places of ministry have similar prayer needs in preparation for our arrival and for the ministry itself. We posted a prayer needs sheet online for our trip to Venezuela in 2006 (page 129). The following Scripture came with an invitation to join in prayer.

"I thank my God every time I remember you. In all my prayers for all of you, I pray with joy because of your partnership in the gospel from the first day until now."

~ PHILIPPIANS 1:3–5

As you join us in prayer, you become a vital member of our team.

THE BOOK OF ACTS

It has become routine now for me to spend about two months prior to a missions trip rereading the Book of Acts. It is a vital part of my preparation for any missions trip. I love to read the history of the spread of Christianity during those 30 years following Jesus' death and resurrection. I am reminded of how significant the power of the Holy Spirit was in empowering those early disciples and witnesses and the direct correlation in today's witnessing.

I would have loved to be present in those early days to hear Peter and John, Stephen, Philip, Paul, Barnabas, Timothy, Silas, John Mark, and all the others proclaim the good news of Jesus Christ. But, Paul is my absolute favorite, and his story is my inspiration for evangelism. To have his boldness is a desire of my heart! He never passed up an opportunity to tell about the saving grace of his Lord and Savior, Jesus Christ. Regardless of circumstances, in spite of threats to his life, in prison or out, Paul was faithful in his witness. He was willing to risk everything for the cause of Christ. He never met a challenge that was too great. I want to be that kind of witness; I want to have total abandonment to Christ.

When I think of Paul, I always go back to his conversion. Here was a man named Saul who was a persecutor of Christians and always a threat to the disciples and their ministry. But, God had other plans. He saw the potential in Saul and called him out. God even had another name for him. The story of Paul's divine encounter with God on the road to Damascus, his subsequent meeting with Ananias, and the fulfillment of the Holy Spirit in his life is absolute inspiration for me.

I was teaching this Scripture to my Sunday School class one morning, filling in for our regular teacher. I wanted to do something different at the end of the lesson to reinforce the Scripture so I took the story and wrote a rap version to sing to the class. I asked the class to clap a rhythm, invited a couple of them to make a rhythmic sound with their voices, and I sang about Paul's conversion experience, his ministry, and his model for us in evangelism.

Hey ~ my name is Paul
An apostle of Christ
Called by Him
Paid for with a price!

I once was lost
And caused great pain
Persecuting Christians
I take all the blame!

The road to Damascus
Was my point in time
When blinded by the Light
God put me in line!

Now I speak for Him
Going place to place
Nothing but the gospel,
Saved by grace!

Now doing good works
And keeping the law
Was nailed to the Cross
Once and for all!

Don't be like Peter
'Cause others to fall
You'll be a hypocrite
And drop the ball!

Stand firm in Christ
Proclaim the good news
Jesus paid it all
And died for you!

Don't cling to the past
And lose your way
The gospel is clear
It is here to stay!

Be true to the gospel
Whatever the cost
Proclaim the good news
And salvation to the lost!

Jew or Gentile
Black or white
We're all the same
In God's precious sight!

CHAPTER 6

BOLDNESS

THE DREAM

I don't know exactly when this dream became a common occurrence in my sleep. Night after night, I had the same dream. I just remember it occurred for the first time following one of my trips to Poland in the late 90s. I kept it to myself for a long time and then shared it only with a couple of friends.

I dreamed I was on the missions field and witnessing to someone. It was so very real and clear in my mind. I was actually there. I would wake up and be talking out loud and continue the witness, going through the steps to bring someone to Christ. The strange thing about this was the realness of my dream. I was actually experiencing it. I would wake myself talking out loud, going over and over how I would bring someone to Christ.

What was this about? I would process and pray, *God, what does this all mean. It must be from You.*

I continued to have the dream and share Christ in my sleep. I would give an invitation and repeat a simple prayer. The dream became more and more frequent. I would wake up and just lie there going over and over the routine.

I cannot remember exactly when it occurred, but one night I realized that God was leading me to a new level of witness and ministry. I had always been comfortable sharing my faith, witnessing, and praying with people to receive Christ. But I felt giving an open invitation to a large group for a response to Christ was for the missionary or pastor on site. I had always passed the large group opportunities off to someone else. God was telling me through this dream that I should do this when the opportunity came. On so many occasions we stood before large groups of children and youth giving testimonies and sharing the gospel. But, I had not always been sensitive to moments when we should be giving an open invitation for all to respond. We talked about God, about who Jesus was in our lives, but we failed in telling them how to have a relationship with Christ and lead them into that relationship. I was burdened by that realization.

This was it! I believe God was saying to me, *Be bold, Betty, and take it all the way. You can give an invitation to the masses. I have equipped you!*

"Do not worry about what to say or how to say it. At that time you will be given what to say, for it will not be you speaking, but the Spirit of your Father speaking through you"

~ MATTHEW 10:19–20

"But the Lord stood at my side and gave me strength, so that through me the message might be fully proclaimed"

~ 2 TIMOTHY 4:17

That revelation through a dream changed my witness. I not only can lead someone to the Living Water, but I can help to give him or her the drink. Now, when I stand before large groups and I feel the Spirit lead, I am comfortable in giving an open invitation. And all this time, I thought doing that was only for ordained ministers. Was I ever wrong! God has ordained me to be a witness through the blood of Jesus and my relationship with Him.

I occasionally still have this dream, but it is no longer a mystery. I see it as God's affirmation of my calling to bring the lost to Christ, reminding me to be bold. I don't worry about what people think. I am not responsible for whether all who pray to receive Christ are serious. I just know that I am to go and tell and give them an opportunity to respond. The Holy Spirit is responsible for the results.

Sometimes I remember missed opportunities when I could have been bolder in my witness. However, I am just grateful for the dream and all the times God woke me up to get His message across to me. It took me a while, but He finally got through to me.

TIME FOR MARY

I noticed Mary sitting alone in the corner of the gym as we gathered the volleyballs and prepared to leave the club on Thursday evening of our May 2007 trip to Rio, Brazil. We had competed against the local team, shared the gospel, and given an invitation to receive Christ. Some of the opposing team and a few fans sitting in the stands had prayed the prayer to accept Christ as Savior. I purposefully stayed behind to be the last one to leave so I could approach Mary.

"Hi, I'm Betty," I said. She introduced herself as Mary. She spoke English.

"You seem very alone and even sad."

"I feel very alone, and I am sad," she responded.

"Tell me, Mary, why you feel like this. Let's talk about it."

Mary told me she was 17 years old and that her friends were out doing things that she just didn't think was right. She did not want to be involved in those activities. I didn't pursue what those things were. I just continued to listen as Mary opened up her heart to me. She told me her parents just didn't understand her, and she couldn't talk to them. This left her feeling very much alone in this world.

> She would never be completely alone again. Jesus would be with her wherever she goes.

"Mary, did you understand what we were talking about just now to the crowd?"

"Yes," she answered.

"Did you pray to ask Jesus into your heart?" I asked her.

She bowed her said and said, "No." Tears began to fall down her cheeks.

"Mary, I care about what you are feeling. Do you wish you had prayed that prayer?"

"Yes," she answered with a nod of the head.

"I can help you do that now," I continued.

"That would be asking too much," she said. "I don't want to keep you. I should have prayed with the group. You have other things to do. It is late."

"Oh, no, Mary! It isn't late. I came all the way from the United States just for this moment with you. Let me help you invite Jesus into your heart. I have all the time we need."

Right then and there Mary prayed with me to receive Christ. I proceeded to tell her that she would never be completely alone again. Jesus would be with her wherever she goes. Our missionary host had stood nearby to listen. She came over and got Mary's name and phone number and told her of a small church nearby that has a number of youth her age. She then called the pastor of this church and the following day he contacted Mary and invited her to church on Sunday. Mary agreed to attend this church the following Sunday. I am confident she met some youth her own age, and she is now in good hands—with Christ and His church.

It was one of those divinely appointed moments that I have grown so accustomed to on these trips; people sitting alone, waiting for someone to be bold enough to reach out, touch, and invite them into a saving relationship with Jesus Christ.

TRUSTING GOD'S CALL

I accepted the call in April 2005 to take a team of basketball players to Venezuela in May 2006. A full year of planning and preparation followed.

Occupying the far northeastern part of South America, Venezuela is bordered by tropics and has only two seasons, the dry season and the rainy season. It has a population of nearly 28 million and a diverse landscape. The rocky Andes Mountains, the Amazon jungle, and white sand beaches are worldwide attractions. Caracas, the capital of Venezuela, and the majority of developed land is situated in the central region. I was excited about experiencing a new part of South America.

In January, prior to our departure in May, I received a call from our travel agent. She told me that because of the ongoing political unrest between Venezuela and the United States all airlines had cancelled flights in and out of Caracas, except for American Airlines. We had tickets on American Airlines to fly into Caracas and then on to our destination in Maturin.

"There is a strong possibility American Airlines will cancel their flights also. You may not get your team into the country. What do you want me to do? Do you want to cancel?" asked our agent.

"Don't cancel us yet" I responded. "I believe God has called us to Venezuela, we have reservations with the only airline that has not been cancelled, and I am just going to trust God to make this trip happen."

I hung up the phone, bowed my head, and asked God to keep our reservations in place for the trip in May. Well, you guessed it. American Airlines continued service in and out of Caracas, Venezuela, as the only airline permitted to enter the country by the Venezuelan government. A lot of people were skeptical about us going, but I felt confident in our call and that God would hold us in His righteous right hand.

Brandon warms up the kids.

We arrived in Caracas on schedule and worked our way through customs while armed guards protected the airport. I had told the team to stay together and not say or do anything that would bring added attention to themselves. However, it is difficult to go unnoticed with a group of basketball players, two of whom stand 6-feet-8-inches and 6-feet-9-inches tall. But, everything went smoothly, as always. It felt like most other airport entry terminals when arriving in a foreign country.

All the kids in the schools where we worked were well aware of the ongoing conflict between the two countries. They could not believe some Americans got into their country, much less in their schools. There were kids who asked, "Do you have guns with you? How did you get in here? Aren't you afraid?" They were concerned for our safety. I know of one school that cancelled our visit due to the uncertainty of the situation. However, before the time was up for us to return home, the school leaders called to see if they could reschedule. We were always made to feel welcomed, and I think they appreciated our willingness to come in spite of the circumstances.

Only once did we encounter some unrest. We had been told that anti-American rallies were routine weekend events in most towns. Supposedly, they were sponsored by the local government to remind the Venezuelan people of the political conflict with the United States. It was Friday, and we were scheduled for an evening session at a local park. We were dressed in uniforms and ready to leave the hotel when our pastor leader called to say the routine Friday night town rally was getting out of hand. The rally was being held near the park we were scheduled to work in so we felt it best to cancel the activities for the evening. That cancellation turned out to be a welcomed relief since we had not had a break all week.

It was an amazing, God-ordained trip of divine appointments. I believe God knew some windows of opportunity were closing and He just wanted to get all He could out of us while we were there.

I have never been afraid on any trips I have taken. There are times when I needed to use my best judgment and make decisions based on circumstances. But, I trust God to lead us to the country and place of ministry, and I trust Him completely to keep us safe. In all my years of leading athletic teams, there has never been a serious injury nor has anyone's safety been in jeopardy.

SALT AND LIGHT

I had a team in Rio, Brazil, in May 2004. We were in our second day of ministry in the *favela* of Rio des Padres. When lunchtime, consisting of the usual beans and rice, was finished, the team ventured back into the afternoon heat for more play, interaction, and ministry.

A couple of people from the local church came seeking help, requesting I go with them into the favela to visit a young woman with two babies. I took Debbie, a member of our team, and an interpreter, and we followed the couple for a 30-minute walk into the heart of this slum. The narrow walkway between homes was somewhat daunting and a little claustrophobic. It was a difficult walk with very little paved area, and we had no clue where we were or how to return if we got lost. We simply followed two locals who knew their way. Open doorways provided a glimpse into small and crowded homes. It was almost as if we were underground.

Upon arrival at our destination, we stepped into the hallway of the home of Sylvanita. I had to stoop low as she escorted us through the door, down a short narrow hallway where we stepped over two sleeping men, and into a very small, dark room. As we pulled the curtain to see the babies, there was no light. We could not see the babies, but we heard them wheezing from obvious bronchial congestion. Someone brought a light bulb from another room, screwed it in the socket, and gave us light. There they lay, six-month-old twin boys. Debbie and I each took a baby and realized quickly that they were very sick. It was so hot and stuffy we could hardly get our breath. I suggested we take the babies and go next door where it was cooler, cleaner, spacious, and lighted. And, I said a prayer, asking God to protect us in case they had something contagious.

> It was so hot and stuffy we could hardly get our breath.

Sylvanita was a single mother, 3,000 miles from her home in northern Brazil, and she was alone. The two sleeping men in the hallway had literally taken her and the babies in from off the street and provided this tiny, dark room where the air was minimal for them to stay. In the States, it would be considered a closet. She told us about the breathing problems of the babies who had been born premature. I requested the young couple take the babies into another room, and Debbie and I proceeded to witness to Sylvanita. She listened as we read Scripture and told her about God's love for her. She shared her story of being so far from home and family, and how alone and afraid she felt. I told Sylvanita that I am single and live alone and sometimes

I get lonely, but I am never alone because Jesus lives in my heart and His presence permeates my home. I told her she could have that same presence and security by inviting Jesus into her heart and life. After a time of loving and caring for Sylvanita, she prayed to receive Christ and rejoiced in the knowledge that she would never be completely alone again. We promised that someone from the local church would follow up and try to provide a place for her to stay and medical care for her babies.

When we stood to leave she said, "Wait!" She left the room, went back to her little space, and brought me what I am sure was her only photograph of her babies, a 5-by-7 framed picture. She cried as she asked me to take the babies' picture home with me to America and remember them. At first, I didn't want to take the photo, not knowing if she had another. But, I did. We all cried together as I accepted the gift. What a precious gift I received from Sylvanita that day!

I had a difficult time going to sleep that night back in my air-conditioned hotel room. I could still hear the congestion from the babies' lungs and see the living conditions. I saw Sylvanita's face changed from loneliness, concern, and fear to joy and peace. I will carry that picture framed in my mind to my grave. And, the framed photograph of those two babies sits beside the desk in my study at home. I am reminded often of the precious gift to me from Sylvanita. I am humbled that God would take me into places like this to be His salt and light to a dark world.

OFF THE BEATEN PATH

People would say that I am a risk-taker, adventurous, spontaneous, and open to new things. Experiences on the missions field have afforded me opportunities for all of the above. In Chile I experienced all of this and so much more. I drove to the top of the Andes Mountains, walked onto the surface of a volcano, drove an ox cart, went to a baptism in a river, and drove deep into the countryside to participate in worship and meetings at rural churches.

I also visited a Mapuche Indian reservation where I drank *mate* *[Mah-The]* with the Indians. The *mate* teacup is a standard custom at most gatherings and visits into homes. An assortment of dried leaves are stuffed into a strainer and boiled water poured over the leaves and through the strainer to make the tea. I had no idea what those leaves were or where they came from. The cup is passed from person to person for a sip of hot tea with a common metal straw usually made of some kind of silver. Yes, we all used the same straw. I enjoyed meals in homes, many times with not a clue as to what was in the pot. I just said a prayer, ate what was before me, and drank from the common metal straw.

I like to see new places. I want to experience as much of the country and the culture as possible. Once while in Santiago, Chile, we took a bus to the coastal city of Viña Del Mar on the Pacific Ocean. Vina is a mixture of Venice, New Orleans, Switzerland, and Florida, a vibrant tourist attraction. Streets were flooded at night with people, buses, and taxis. However, within two blocks of the city is poverty staring you in the face. We took a bus as far as it would go into the hillside, and then took another one out. We went up and down the coast, stopping along the way to talk with the people and hand out tracts that told about the gospel and how to have a personal relationship with Jesus Christ.

Other times, Clara, the missionary, drove an old blue station wagon that rattled a lot. It reminded me of the station wagon I drove that summer in high school to take Elvira to work with Mexican migrant workers. Clara's car was filled with bags of goodies: food, clothes, books, tracts, and more. I named it Old Blue. We drove into the country to visit people in faraway churches. As we saw people walking, we stopped to hand out tracts in Spanish and talk about Jesus. Of course Clara did all the talking. It was then that I understood why I had taken two years of Spanish as a Belmont student. I would give greetings with my limited Spanish, and as time passed, the language became more familiar to me. I couldn't make a good sentence, but I could communicate. God prepares us for what is to come. Sometimes on our car trips, we would need to stop and use an outhouse or just a tree for a shield. None of that bothered me because I grew up using an outdoor toilet.

I had an international driver's license and drove Old Blue on occasions. I got carried away one day and was stopped by the policia for speeding. I rolled down the window, put on the nicest smile I could muster, and I said, *"Buenos dias, Señor."* He was surprised to see a tall, blonde, American woman sitting behind the wheel, speaking Spanish. He smiled and asked to see my license. After studying it and flirting a little bit he waved me on my way, speaking a few words of Spanish. I think he told me to slow down.

> Sometimes it is off the beaten path that we have our most unique and meaningful moments.

I did attract a lot of attention: tall, blonde, female, and American. I never saw another female as tall as me, 5-feet-11-inches. The men were short, too. In churches, I tried to find a seat near the side so I wouldn't block everybody's view. When I stood, it was even worse!

Regardless of where I have been (Chile, Scotland, Poland, Costa Rica, Portugal, Brazil, Venezuela, Ukraine, South Africa, Malta) or where God takes me in the future, I want to keep this same adventurous spirit and boldness to see and experience all He has in store for me. Sometimes it is off the beaten path that we have our most unique and meaningful moments.

A SENSE OF URGENCY

It was Thursday night, May 15, 2008, in Rio, Brazil, following our long evening of exhibition, clinics, demonstrations, and play with a local club team. About 30 young men from ages 20 to 25 sat before us and listened to two of our team members tell about their relationship with Jesus Christ and the impact that their Savior has in their lives. It was a perfect lead-in to one of the most powerful times of sharing the gospel I have ever experienced. Their obvious connection to God's Word moved me with great passion as I listened to some of them pray to receive Christ. Here were big, Brazilian basketball players hanging onto every word being spoken. And, God's Word did not come up void.

Following our session, the players continued to hang around. I asked Nilton, a tall and beautiful Brazilian young man, "Do you have this relationship with Jesus that we have talked about?"

He shook his head like *I don't know* and said, "I go to church."

I proceeded to tell him that the Bible says nothing about the church forgiving our sins and giving us eternal life. Only Jesus can do that. It wasn't long until I said, "Nilton, I want to give you another opportunity to pray to receive Christ. Would you like that?"

With a tear in his eye, he responded, "Yes, please."

We prayed together and Nilton ask Jesus into his heart. With a smile as big as the ocean he said, "Thank you. I know what I just did." Then he gave me a hug that said it all.

I looked around and there were seven or eight guys just standing there watching, like they were waiting for something. I could not walk away from them. You see, I just knew they were waiting for Jesus. I proceeded to ask them if they had understood what we had said, and if they had prayed the prayer.

"I go to church," one responded. Another said, "I go sometimes." Another said, "I just don't know." But they didn't walk away. They were waiting to hear more.

My heart was breaking. I was moved with compassion and love for these big old athletes who needed a Savior. I felt an urgency to talk to them. I said, "Hey guys, listen to me. This is not about religion or going to church; it is about a relationship." I continued to share the gospel, and finally I said, "We are going to leave you in a few minutes. I do not want to leave you without Christ. Won't you reconsider?

You may never have another opportunity. You aren't doing this for me. You must choose for yourselves."

They began nodding their heads and drawing a little closer into the circle. With tears in my eyes, a smile on my face, and a deep connection to them in my heart, I listened as all of those guys prayed aloud to accept Christ as their Lord and Savior. I had just had an encounter with the amazing saving grace of Jesus Christ!

Later that night, on the bus going back to the hotel, one of our team members said to me, "I would have been intimidated to talk to those big basketball players like you did. You are so bold and courageous."

I responded, "They are just like you, young adult men who play basketball. The only difference is they speak a different language and are a few years older. They needed someone to introduce them to Jesus just like someone did for you."

WILL TAKES THE LEAD

The normal routine for sharing the gospel on our sports evangelism trips is for a couple of the athletes to give greetings and testimonies to set the stage for the presentation of the gospel. I always try to "piggyback" off their sharing and go right into the gospel presentation. Through the years, there have been some students that I thought could give a clear presentation of the gospel and maybe an open invitation to the crowd. But, for someone who has never done that before a crowd, it is pretty overwhelming and intimidating.

In 2006 in Anaco, Venezuela, we had completed a session of play and interaction for a group of maybe 400 to 500 students at a local school. I had invited Will Peeples to give his testimony. I stood amazed as he took his witness to another level. He then turned the session over to me for summarizing the gospel and giving an invitation.

Following the session, I told him, "Will, you can do what I do. You came ever so close today. I want you to think about it, pray about it, and tomorrow I would like you to do my part."

"I don't know," he said. "You really think I could handle that?"

"Of course you can. You were ready to do it today, coming ever so close. Just be bold. You just need to think ahead and prepare yourself to lead them to accept Christ."

"I'll think about it," he said.

I prayed for Will that night that God would give him the desire and the courage to step forward to the challenge and a new level of sharing.

The next morning he said, "I'll do it. Just pray for me."

"I already have, Will," I responded, "and I will be praying while you lead."

Will stepped up that day and provided a powerful closing to the

{ God will remind you of these moments. }

testimony time, sharing the gospel and giving an invitation, the first time one of our student-athletes had done this. He didn't miss a beat. An echo rang in the air as a large number of kids prayed with him to receive Christ. I had tears in my eyes as I watched and listened to him. When he turned to me following the response I gave him a big hug and said, "How does it feel, Will?"

"Awesome," he said, with a smile running from ear to ear. "I never experienced anything like that before."

"Good," I responded. "I want you to do it again in the morning."

I wanted to reinforce what he had done by allowing him to experience it once again. He did it again the next day and received another wonderful response. It was a little different, as it always is. Each crowd is unique, and sometimes keeping their attention is difficult. He did great, but felt he had not done as well as the day before.

He said, "You really have to stay focused, don't you, regardless of circumstances. I don't know how you do it so much. You cannot let your thoughts stray."

I said, "Will, the more you do this the easier it gets. You have reached a milestone in your Christian life. You'll never be the same. God will remind you of these moments in the days, weeks, and years ahead. I can assure you it will be a highlight in your Christian walk."

And, I watched his teammates give him high-fives and hugs of congratulations and affirmation for what he had just done.

Will experienced something in Venezuela that very few young men his age ever do. He proclaimed the gospel and brought a crowd of people to profess Christ as Lord and Savior. I trust this was just the beginning for him. When I saw him following the trip I asked if he had shared that experience with his mom and dad.

"I did," he responded. "They were proud of me."

Of course they were. Wouldn't any mother and father embrace their child who demonstrates such boldness in serving Christ!

CHAPTER 7

PASSION

The word *passion* denotes a strong feeling and emotion, desire, belief in, and deep love for something. It is a compelling force from within that drives a person to action. It is unbridled enthusiasm, sometimes resulting in outrageous expression. It is a commitment to something greater than ourselves. It can drive one to the heights and depths of despair or to our very best potential. We all have a passion for something.

Observing Passion Week helps us remember the arrest, torture, death, crucifixion, burial, and ultimately the resurrection of Jesus Christ. In 1980 I had the privilege of seeing the "Passion Play," a dramatic representation of the passion of Christ that is given once every ten years in the Bavarian village of Oberammergau, Germany. The film *The Passion of the Christ* is a dramatic and graphic depiction of Christ's sufferings leading to His subsequent death on the Cross. Christ's passion and commitment to His calling and purpose is the ultimate demonstration of passion!

I have had the privilege of working with some passionate people through the years on the missions field, people who have literally given their lives and very being to share the good news of Jesus Christ. Team participants have caught the passion and dared to follow the examples in their own journey. In this chapter I'd like to share the stories of a few of those people.

WHATEVER IT TAKES IN RIO: ELIZABETH OATES

Elizabeth Oates was one of a kind! Her 42 years on the missions field was a lifetime of service. Our team of basketball players grew to love her and her heart for the people of Rio, especially the people in the slums. We knew Elizabeth would be leaving the missions field in November following our trip in August 1999. She would take her last furlough and then retire as a career missionary.

Elizabeth settled back into life in the States during her furlough. She came to Nashville and spent several days in my home. I brought her to Belmont where she attended our women's basketball game and yelled for her team. She had recurring cancer, and on the first official day of her retirement, Elizabeth left this earth and went to her home in heaven. I wrote the following tribute to Elizabeth when a conflict kept me from attending her funeral.

Elizabeth Oates was a giant of a woman to me, an inspiration from the first day I met her in Brazil in August 1999. We had an instant connection. I loved her heart, her heart for the people of Brazil. I loved her tenacity, her spunk! She had so much energy and enthusiasm.

I marveled at her passion for sharing Christ. I felt a kindred spirit with Elizabeth. She could laugh with us, play with us, and she cried with me as we drove away from her "favorite" slum, which became my favorite slum. In that particular slum, I remember we were guarded by the police with guns as we played on an outdoor court. The police were stationed on top of concrete walls that separated the school from the streets of the slum. I wasn't afraid because Elizabeth wasn't afraid!

Elizabeth Oates and Betty share the gospel with a young man on a missions trip.

She was held in high esteem everywhere we went. The television cameras became her platform for telling the real reason why the basketball team was in Brazil. The radio personnel interviewed her about the American team, and she planted more seeds for Christ. I would watch her on the bus as we traveled from place to place, eyes closed, catching a quick nap for more energy. She was an amazing leader-teacher-example as she coordinated our two weeks of ministry.

Elizabeth had never worked with a sports team, but it didn't take her long to catch on and feel right at home with a basketball team.

It was my privilege to have her visit in my home when she returned to the States for her final furlough. She spent the day with me at Belmont. I took her to share with a small group of trustees who were on campus. She affirmed Belmont's commitment to our sports evangelism program.

I had an early afternoon appointment. She said, "I'm going to walk around campus." She didn't return. I set out looking for her. I could not find her. About 30 minutes later, she came up with some of the basketball girls. She had run into a couple of them on campus and had been to their pregame meal. Was I surprised? No, that was Elizabeth, spontaneous and open to opportunity to love, encourage, and minister! We went to see the girls play that evening. She was a nervous wreck, cheering them every step of the way to a victory. We came home from the game exhausted.

We all loved her. She was "Miss Elizabeth" to our team. We were all saddened to hear of her death. She was an ordinary woman with an extraordinary heart for ministry.

Elizabeth won the ultimate victory. She played the game of life with great intensity, integrity, passion, and humility. She was a consummate teammate, team leader, and servant. She touched my life in those two weeks. She made a difference in the lives of 12 college basketball players and 2 coaches. Her life lives on in countless others through her 40-plus years of service and ministry. I count it all joy to have known her, to love her, and share ministry with her.

Infectious Excitement in Chile: Clara Brincefield Huff

Retired career missionary, Clara Brincefield Huff, comes to mind when I think about the word *passion*. Her passion for missions, enthusiasm, and excitement for ministry is infectious, and her laughter contagious. Maybe it is her voice that comes through loud and clear as she communicates. Maybe it's the energy with which she speaks; her mannerisms, volume, and clarity of words. Maybe it's the Spanish language itself! Whatever it is, Clara is excitement in the truest sense of the word. She loves Spanish-speaking people. It doesn't matter where they are from. If they speak Spanish, they are her family; she connects with them; and she becomes the ultimate communicator.

My experiences with Clara on the missions field in Chile would prove life changing for me. I saw firsthand through Clara what commitment to missions and excitement about sharing the gospel are all about. Clara lived out the Great Commission and her calling to the missions field with a passion I had never witnessed before. She was my host on my first overseas missions experience, and I learned from one of the very best!

Clara could get more out of a 24-hour day than anyone I had ever known. She loved people unconditionally, and she never met a stranger. Her excitement and boldness in reaching out and sharing the gospel was astounding. She never saw a challenge that she could not fulfill. She coordinated volunteer teams that ranged from medical to construction to women's camps to prayer retreats and on and on.

Betty with Clara.

She would teach children, draw up church plans for construction crews, bargain for materials, preach at the drop of a hat, and even dance a jig to share the culture. Her energy level was unbelievable. She was the missionary version of the Energizer bunny that just keeps going and going. And, she would work herself into complete exhaustion.

Going with her in the old station wagon—Old Blue—into the countryside to witness and hand out tracts was a rare treat. It was on those occasions that I experienced the country and the people in their natural surroundings. I saw and went places that the regular volunteer did not experience.

> I can close my eyes and feel like I am revisiting Chile.

Clara retired as a career missionary after 32 years of service in Chile. Her last furlough was spent in Nashville at Belmont University as missionary in residence. She and I shared a home in Brentwood for a year. It was during this time that she met the man of her dreams, Reverend L. M. Huff, a retired pastor, director of missions, and widower from Kentucky. They married and shared a home and ministry in Donelson, Tennessee, near Nashville, with Spanish-speaking people until he died of recurring cancer six years later. Clara now lives in Wilmington, North Carolina, near family, where she continues to work with Spanish-speaking people. She is a member of a Spanish church, teaches Bible study, and has a class in English as a second language. Most days you will find her somewhere other than home, speaking and doing ministry. And, you guessed it, she still returns regularly to her beloved Chile for special events, personal vacations, and with volunteer teams to do special projects.

When Clara comes to visit in my home, I spend a lot of time answering the phone in Spanish as all her friends call for "Miss Clara." When she takes the phone, there is excitement in the air. Some of the calls are from Chile and her beloved Chilean friends. During those calls, for a moment, I can close my eyes and feel like I am revisiting Chile. Clara is another in a long line of missionaries that

I have served with in the field. The energy, enthusiasm, and excitement with which she served and still serves cannot be described in any other word but passion!

JOURNEY TO CHRIST IN POLAND: JEREMY KEES

In 1997, I was in Poland for the third year in a row with a basketball team. On a long train ride from Tarnow in south Poland back to Warsaw for the trip home, one of the players, Jeremy Kees, was writing in his journal. I asked about his journal, and he invited me to read some of what he had written.

I discovered that he had asked Jesus into his heart during the week. Jeremy wrote that he had thought he was a Christian, but found he had never asked Jesus into his heart. That week in Tarnow, Poland, was the beginning of a new life for Jeremy. His excitement for his newfound faith was refreshing. He couldn't wait to tell his girlfriend, Brooke. Jeremy would accompany me the next two years on more missions trips. His testimony was fresh and real and exciting for him to share.

> Others might be taking a nap to catch up on their sleep, but not Jeremy.

Jeremy loved to travel. He saw more than any other team member, taking in the world with a passion. Others might be taking a nap to catch up on their sleep, but not Jeremy. He was observing, soaking in the world. Prospective graduates must fill out a questionnaire before graduation from Belmont; I was told that Jeremy wrote that his most memorable experiences at Belmont were his missions trips, especially the first trip to Poland where he gave his heart to Christ.

Jeremy married Brooke after graduating from Belmont. He later earned his master's and doctoral degrees in business and marketing, and is now a university professor. Jeremy and Brooke have a son, Jace, and a daughter, Hallie.

Jeremy has a passion for sharing his faith. He leads a weekly Bible study on his campus. I can't wait to see where God is taking him. We still regularly keep in touch, and he continues to support our sports evangelism ministry. He has come a long way in the past ten years, from when his journey with Christ began in the faraway country of Poland.

POWER COUPLE IN BRAZIL: SHARON AND RAY FAIRCHILD

Complete opposites is how I would characterize this missionary couple! Three decades on the missions field together in Brazil requires balance, and God certainly blessed them with that in their marriage.

Ray is laid back and easy going with a dry wit and sense of humor. He never saw a book he didn't like, surrounding himself with books of all kinds and a library that keeps any and all kinds of information at his fingertips at a moment's notice. A soft and gentle voice complements his pleasant demeanor. He's an expert at writing materials on evangelism to be used in missions, planting churches, and supporting Sharon as she leads volunteer teams from the United States who come to serve.

Now Sharon is a different breed or "a horse of a different color" kind of person. She is take-charge and hands-on in every sense of the words. I would say she is driven and has a sense of urgency as she coordinates team after team of

Ray is in good company.

volunteers who come for ministry in and around Rio. When she speaks, she commands attention. You'll find her direct without being confrontational. She speaks as a person who has authority. Sharon is comfortable organizing a medical clinic and working in

Sharon tries her hand at basketball.

the pharmacy, planning a citywide evangelism effort, coordinating a sports evangelism itinerary, leading youth in door-to-door evangelism, hammering away on a building project, and discipling and mentoring a team of local translators who are the best I have experienced in all my missions endeavors.

Ray and Sharon are gifts from God to one another. Their love and depth of companionship is evident as they allow one another the gift of space and support in all they do. The demands they put on one another are light and easy. They operate in total freedom, enjoying one another's support and encouragement. They are blessed with three sons who are all college graduates, successful, and still supportive of their parents' work, joining them on the field to serve whenever their schedules permit.

What a joy and privilege to serve with this couple and share in their lifelong commitment and passion for service. They retired in 2009 and returned to the States where they were initially on staff as missionaries-in-residence at my church, Brentwood Baptist, in Brentwood, Tennessee. Ray is now on staff there as Connection minister, and I know God will use their gifts of missions and evangelism as they serve Him in the local church. And, I will be blessed to continue my friendship and partnership in missions with them.

TRANSLATOR PAR EXCELLENCE IN UKRAINE: VLADIMIR

R egardless of where you are, communication is a key to one's success in sharing the gospel. We have been blessed through the years to have good translators available. I can remember some trips early in this ministry where we had difficulty communicating because of the language barrier. It became more and more important when scheduling these sports missions trips that there be enough translators available so that we did not miss opportunities to communicate.

I can recall many good translators, but one in particular stands out as I think back to the people who have stood by my side to become my voice, my heart, my passion for Christ.

I met Vladimir when I took a team to the Ukraine in 2005. "Vlady" was 31 years old, married, and the father of two small children. He was our main translator during our two-week stay. He bonded instantly with the college students and became one of our team. He was our constant companion throughout the ministry. I was so comfortable when he translated for me, especially when sharing the gospel and asking people to respond by receiving Christ. He became an extension of my very being: my voice, my heart, and my soul. Before a sentence was out of my mouth, he began translation.

> From that moment on Vlady called me Mama.

He was at the hotel each morning to share breakfast and stayed with us late into the evening, until he had translated our order for breakfast the next morning. He shared with us at lunch one day that his mother practically disowned him when he married, telling him that he could do better. She called him a stupid boy. Tears rolled down his cheeks as he told of this painful moment in his life. He clearly missed having a supportive mother in his life. I responded with, "Vlady, if I had a son it would please me if he were just like you." Well, from that moment on Vlady called me Mama, and he is forever etched in my soul.

I discovered during our time there that he had to walk two miles a day from his home to meet us. We then began to get him a trolley or cab to and from home to our hotel. Vlady had never owned a car and looked forward to the day he would have one for his family.

Vlady taught in a local school, attended seminary, and preached on Sundays. He came to get us that first Sunday in a suit that obviously was mixed and matched from a place where the people go to get handouts. His shoes were a size too large. He had told us he has to wear a suit and tie every day to teach. I had taken some extra money to use as I saw a need. So, on Tuesday I gave Vlady some money and told him to buy a new suit of clothes. He was hesitant, but finally agreed to accept my offer. The guys on our team agreed to take him and help pick out his new clothes. They came back with a new suit, shirt, tie, belt, socks, and shoes. He was so proud. He told the guys he had never owned any new piece of clothing in his entire life. I later found that he took the extra money left over and bought his son a new pair of tennis shoes, which was the child's first new clothing as well.

Vladimir and his beautiful family.

Finally it was time for us to return to the States. We gathered early—1:00 A.M.—in our hotel's small lobby to begin our journey home. We had a two-hour bus ride to Kiev to catch our flight to the United States. To our surprise, Vlady was waiting for us in the lobby. He was dressed in his new suit of clothes, and he was smiling from ear to ear. We had said good-bye to him the day before, but he wanted to thank us one more time for loving him and reaching out to him. Everyone stopped and surrounded him with hugs and kisses and love. He had touched each of us deeply, and we would never forget him. I will always remember the last words he said to me as I hugged him good-bye. He said, "I love you, Mama."

Vladimir had a passion for sharing the good news of Jesus Christ. When he spoke, you knew it was coming from the depths of his heart. When I raised or lowered my voice in sharing, he did the same to catch the passion, the intensity of the moment and statement. His life is one of sacrifice and service. I continue to get emails from Vlady and occasionally a photo of him and his family. He has graduated from seminary and been ordained into the ministry. I may never see Vlady again, but I am confident we will be reunited again one day in heaven. And, he will bring many people with him because of his passion for sharing Christ.

A Rap? For Me?

In 2004, after I was inducted into the Tennessee Sports Hall of Fame, my Sunday School class honored me with a surprise celebration. Along with class members, several guests were invited to share greetings and make presentations. Brentwood Mayor, Anne Dunn, made a surprise appearance and presented me with a key to the city. Obviously, I was overwhelmed with the love, affection, and heartfelt appreciation shown me by my sisters in Christ. I will always remember that wonderful afternoon of celebration.

The following rap song, written by class member Jane Simpson, was sung to me by four fun-loving class members, who were decked out in Belmont basketball uniforms borrowed from the athletic department. I share it with you, with Jane's permission, because it expresses my passion for sharing Christ.

THE BW RHAPSODY

By Jane Simpson

WE ALL KNOW BETTY,
SHE'S #1.
AND SHE'S LOTS OF FUN.

SHE CAN TEACH AND PRAY
AND SING, IT'S TRUE!
WHY, SHE'LL EVEN COME OVER
AND RAP WITH YOU!!

WITH A BASKETBALL,
SHE'S MADE A NAME.
BUT SHARING THE WORD
IS REALLY HER GAME.

IN THE GUISE OF A COACH
SHE'S TRAVELED THE WORLD,
SHOWING GOD'S LOVE
TO EVERY BOY AND GIRL.

HER SUITCASE IS FULL
OF BASKETBALL GEAR...
(THE TOOLS SHE USES
TO CATCH A KID'S EAR)

SHE TEACHES THEM A SKILL
AND THEIR JUMP SHOT IMPROVES,
BUT THE REAL PLAY BEGINS
WHEN THE SPIRIT MOVES.

BETTY KNOWS HER MISSION
RIGHT FROM THE START...
DRIBBLE THAT BALL
WHILE GOD CHANGES A HEART!!

NOW, WHEN WE ALL GET TO HEAVEN
AND START LOOKING 'ROUND,
WE'RE LIKELY TO HEAR
AN EAR-PIERCING SOUND!

IS IT A PLANE OR A TRAIN
OR A PATRIOT MISSILE?
NO, IT'S BETTY WISEMAN
BLOWING HER WHISTLE.

SHE'S GOING FOR THE GOAL
AND IT'S EASY TO SEE,
WHY, ON THE JESUS TEAM,
SHE'S AN MVP!!!

CHAPTER 8

A CONNECTION FOR LIFE: MARIA MEETS JESUS

I met Maria in May 2004 in Rio, Brazil, on an outdoor basketball court that sits on one of the highest hills in Costa Barros. It was the first of two days on this court when I noticed a very thin Brazilian woman outside the fence, holding a baby. She was dressed as all the others for the hot sun in shorts, halter-top, and flip-flops. I can tell you right now that Rio, Brazil, is the flip-flop capital of the world. Seldom did we see a pair of shoes, only flip-flops.

I kept watching this woman and soon discovered that she had a little girl participating in the clinic. Finally, I approached her and reached out to touch the baby that was nursing. I have learned that paying attention to a baby or small child with a parent instantly opens the door for conversation. She literally took this nursing baby from her breast and handed him to me with a smile. I was moved that she would do that. He looked to be several months old. I was used to the fact that it isn't unusual for babies to nurse for one to two years in other countries.

I called for one of the translators and learned that her name was Maria, and that the baby was one year old. I invited her to listen to our players who were, at the moment, sharing the gospel in small groups. I walked around with the sleeping baby and cared for him so she could be free to listen. He was quite heavy as healthy one year olds can be, but I was determined that she have an opportunity to hear our team members share. She stood behind the group of kids seated on the hot concrete court and listened intently.

When the session concluded, Maria continued to follow the team and children around, watching her daughter participate. I still held the baby while walking around the court and giving some instructions. It was late afternoon, and we were readying to leave the court and prepare for the evening worship service. I was beginning to think I would have to take this baby home with me. But, Maria came for her baby and said she would be back for more the next day.

The following morning I realized we were going to another court in another part of the town, and I kind of panicked when I thought about Maria. I knew she said she would be back, but now we were relocating. I just said, *"OK, God, bring Maria to us."*

The word was out and news had traveled about the Americans and basketball. It didn't take long for the court at the new location to fill with people. I had been working the crowd again, witnessing to some adults. I looked up and there stood Maria with her baby. She had found us! I whispered, *"Thank you, God."* The baby was asleep in her arms. I walked over, took the child from her once again, and she listened to the sharing. I walked around and cared for the sleeping baby while Maria heard more about Jesus.

Right: Betty meets Maria and her baby. A translator stood by to help. Below: Holding Maria's sleeping baby.

When the session ended, I asked Maria if I could talk to her. I took a translator, and we went to a quiet spot, removed from the crowd, to share the gospel and witness to her. As I sat with her, I held the sleeping child, and Maria asked Jesus into her heart. I had prayed for this moment for two days. Another divine appointment! I introduced her to Pastor Douglas. He spent some time with her, invited her to church, and Maria promised me she would see me at church that night. I gave her a Portuguese New Testament and wrote a note to her on the first page. I introduced her to our team and told them about her decision to follow Christ. I wanted to give her something personal from me, so I took off my earrings and gave them as a gift of myself.

That night I was sitting in this makeshift church on the side of the road, literally on the sidewalk of the street of this slum. We were singing, and someone tapped me on the shoulder. I turned around to see the most beautiful Brazilian woman I had ever seen. Maria? Yes, it was Maria! I hardly recognized her. She looked radiant; and her smile said it all. I could not believe my eyes. She had come! I observed her and held her hand as she listened and watched intently, not knowing what to do or how to act, then slowly she begin to participate in the singing and worship experience. The transformation took place before my very eyes. I watched the joy of her newfound Jesus erupt from her very soul as her smile told the story. She shared with me afterwards that she had never been in a church, but she promised the pastor she would be back. She had found a new family and church home. She lived a good distance from the church, but Pastor Douglas promised to pick her up in his car.

Maria found Jesus on the hill that day in the hot sun of Rio de Janeiro, in a very unlikely place, on a basketball court. I could not get Maria out of my mind. She was in my heart and a part of me forever. She and I would be connected for life. God was showing me some things on this trip. He was telling me to venture outside the box, outside the court, and into the crowds. He was saying, *Do whatever it takes to connect with people, even if it means tending to a baby for two days.* He had divine appointments waiting for me. I didn't know if I would ever see Maria again on earth, but I was confident we would be reunited again someday in heaven. Her smile and the joy in her newfound Jesus were embedded in my very soul.

It was very difficult to say good-bye to Maria and to so many others that night as we left Costa Barros. We would not return, moving to yet another part of Rio the following day. Maria stayed at my side throughout the evening, and we hugged and cried when I stepped onto the bus. I was leaving a part of myself behind. She was my sister in Christ.

It took me a very long time to go to sleep that night. I lay in bed and literally wept for all the Marias in Rio and around the world who are waiting for someone to share Jesus. I would never be the same, and my ministry in sports evangelism would never be the same. God had used Maria to teach me yet something else. I remembered the Scripture in Acts that I had read the day prior to leaving on this particular trip. It was the Scripture of Philip's divine appointment with the Ethiopian eunuch. I remembered how I had prayed early that Sunday morning that God would give me divine appointments in Rio. No wonder I was moved to tears!

A New Church Start

The summer following the 2004 trip to Rio, missionaries Sharon and Ray Fairchild were in Tennessee for a visit to the Tennessee Baptist Convention and local churches that had partnered with them for projects in Rio. While here they told me about Pastor Douglas discovering a corner piece of property in Maria's community that was for sale, thinking it would be the perfect place to build a church. I inquired about the price for the land and was told it would cost between $300 and

> I wept for all the Marias in Rio and around the world.

$400 in American dollars. Imagine that! I immediately sat down, wrote them a personal check for $500 and told them to buy the property.

The story continued one year later when I received a CD that showed photos of Pastor Douglas, Sharon, and Ray standing on the foundation of the new church that was being built in Maria's community. They kept me posted during the months ahead, sharing with me the progress of the building of this new church start.

In the summer of 2006, I spoke with Sharon by phone in Rio where she was working with a medical team in that same community. She said, "Oh, Betty, guess who I just saw and talked to about 15 minutes ago? She was asking if her friend, Betty, was here."

Above: Start of a new church.
Right: Ray surveys the site.

"Who would that be?" I asked.

"Your friend, Maria," Sharon responded. "If you had called just a little bit earlier you could have spoken with her. She had your picture in her hand, asking if you were here with the medical team."

Unbelievable! I was speechless and tears came to my eyes. Maria remembered me! And, a church was being built in her community. She would be a member. God was still working in that favela and in Maria's life. It now became my heart's desire to revisit Costa Barros, go to the new church start, and reconnect with Maria.

Alone in Rio

Fast forward now to May 2007 and I am back in Rio with the volleyball team and coaches from Belmont, competing with local club teams, visiting schools, and doing ministry. It was my first trip using volleyball as the platform for sharing Christ. The ten days of ministry far exceeded any expectations I had for this particular team.

I had made plans to send the team back to the United States with their coaches, and I would remain in Rio, alone in the hotel, to connect with a medical team coming in from my local church two days following. I would be in Rio in a hotel by myself for two days and nights between the two ministries. I had stayed at that particular hotel on three trips, so the thought of staying alone there a couple of days was no big deal. However, when the time came for me to watch the volleyball team go through security at the airport without me, to begin their journey home, I was a little unsettled. I began to have second thoughts. This was my first time to do something like this.

One of our translators took me back to the hotel in a cab. Due to heavy work traffic, it took us well over an hour to get back to the hotel. I had a nice visit with the translator, but all the while, I was thinking about the team on their way home. Why had I made a commitment to stay an extra week, especially with two nights alone in a hotel? Upon arrival back at the hotel, I made my way to a sandwich shop on the roof and ordered a burger and fries for dinner. The waiter spoke no English, but he knew me from previous times during the past two weeks I had been there for a sandwich. He just smiled as I ordered, sitting alone with my thoughts. I'm sure he must have thought, *Where are the other team members?*

> I was a little unsettled. I began to have second thoughts.

It was still rather early, but I retired to my room, took a shower, prayed for a safe flight for the team, and fell asleep, exhausted from two weeks of volleyball and ministry. Twelve hours later I awoke, rested, and in no rush to get up and go somewhere. I took my time getting dressed then spent the morning at the Internet café, reading the online journal kept as an update about our trip by our coaches and players. It did my heart good to read, for the first time, their entries of thoughts and reflections of experiences during the past two weeks. And, I had spent my first night alone in another country and felt safe and secure in God's care.

REUNITED

The phone rang in my room around noon and a translator, greeted me.

"Betty, we are here to take you to Costa Barros to see Pastor Douglas and find Maria." Are you kidding me? What a surprise! I got so excited!

Sharon and Ray had arranged for two volunteers and the translator to drive me to this favela to see if we could find Maria. Their thoughtfulness touched me. I gathered some items and prepared a gift bag just in case I found Maria.

It took us about an hour to get to Costa Barros and the church where we had worked three years previous. Pastor Douglas was there to meet us. It was so good to see him, revisit the church, and see the renovations and remodeling done since our visit in 2004.

He said, "Let me take you to the church that stands on the property you bought for us."

We all piled in the car and headed for the church. As we made the turn onto the side road leading up that long quarter-mile hill it all came back to me. There would be a little fenced in basketball court at the top awaiting us. Slowly we climbed. At least this time we were in a car. Each previous time I'd been on top of this hill I had walked with basketball players, carrying basketballs and supplies, breathing hard and heavy. As we neared the crest of the hill there it was, the little court! Memories flooded my mind of the day we had spent on that court three years earlier. I could still see the kids, the people who had come to observe, and then my thoughts turned to Maria!

"Pastor Douglas, do you know where Maria lives?" I asked.

"No," he said. "I just know she lives somewhere on this hill. We'll ask if anyone knows her."

Now, it is a really big hill. We would be looking for a needle in a haystack!

I had brought with me an 8-by-10 photo that was taken of Maria, me, the baby, and the translator the moment when Maria had prayed

Clockwise from top left:
Ray shows the contractors
the church plans he drew.
Sharon reviews the newly
poured concrete. Columns
are erected. The church
takes shape.

to receive Christ. I had prayed for an opportunity to give it to her personally. I held it tightly, yet reverently. That photo held precious memories.

We left the car parked and walked across the way to the church, a new building completed only within the past year, born out of our ministry in 2004. Pastor Douglas first walked us through the small building and talked about the ministry. It was good to be in the new church. It was not furnished, simple in structure, but born out of my relationship with Maria.

We showed the photo to some people near the church, but no one recognized Maria. We moved on, showing the photo to other people as we walked. Then we met two children. When they saw the photo, they pointed to the tiny homes across the dirt pathway and said, "I think she lives over there." I was getting excited. As we walked from the church and looked across the way, a young girl came out of a small shack on that big hill. When she saw me she yelled, "Beh-Chi"! It was Maria's daughter, the one who participated in the basketball clinic. She ran back into the house and moments later out came Maria. It was Maria! I had found her! I was overcome with emotions!

We had a wonderful reunion with lots of hugs, love, and some tears. I gave her the photo and asked, "Do you remember this day?"

"Yes," she said. "I remember. I can't believe you came back."

"I came back to see you, Maria. I have remembered you and prayed for you all this time. I wanted to see you again."

She told us to wait as she went inside and brought out another baby, a new baby. She proudly handed me her newborn son. We spent about 30 minutes together as I held the child and talked to her through the translator and Pastor Douglas, who speaks both English and Portuguese. We all gathered around, and I prayed for Maria and her three children. (The little baby boy I'd held three years earlier must have been asleep inside I think).

I thanked God for our sweet reunion and for the church He had provided in Maria's community.

Now, it was time to leave. I hugged Maria and said my good-byes. It wasn't as difficult to leave her as it had been three years earlier. I knew where she lived now and that she had a church right next door. God had granted me the desire of my heart, to see Maria once again. She had Jesus in her heart, and now she had the new church start in her neighborhood. She would have the photo of us to remind her of the moment she came to know Jesus. I left with perfect peace in my heart. The second night alone in Rio was a time of celebration, praise, and rejoicing in God's goodness to me. And now I knew why I had made the decision to remain in Rio, alone, those two days and nights, between ministries. I'm still praising God for that wonderful and divinely orchestrated reunion with Maria. Her story illustrates why I do what I do. To God be the glory!

> She ran back into the house and moments later out came Maria. It was Maria! I had found her!

CHAPTER 9

WHAT ABOUT YOU?

I trust the experiences shared in this book have served to motivate, encourage, and inspire you to action. You have a platform! Mine is sports. What is yours? Is God calling you to volunteer for a missions trip, maybe your first? Will you take the plunge and dive off that platform like I did and say yes to His call, allowing Him to show you things you cannot learn or experience sitting on a church pew or in a Sunday School classroom?

Sometimes I think about all the years I thought about going on a missions trip, but just never had the courage. The questions that went through my mind: What can I do? How can I take time away from my work? How can I afford this? And, the fear of not knowing what to say, not being confident in my ability to share Christ.

The college athletes who've traveled with me will tell you their experiences in sports evangelism on the missions field changed their lives. It caused them to take a look at their relationship with Christ and all that means to them now and in their future. You can bet they were anxious prior to their first trip. They probably asked the same questions that I did. However, they trusted me to steer them in the right direction and to lead them along the way. And they saw, just like I did, that when God calls and we are faithful to say yes to His call, He will equip us for service.

Today, I am claiming Isaiah 41:9–10 for you, the reader: *"I took you from the ends of the earth, from its farthest corners I called you. I said, 'You are my servant'; I have chosen you.... So do not fear, for I am with you; do not be dismayed, for I am your God. I will strengthen you and help you; I will uphold you with my righteous right hand."*

Won't you heed that tugging on your heart and say yes to the call? I encourage you to take the next step of faith and—***Go!***

Is God calling you? He will be with you and provide for your needs. Do not fear! Be a short-term volunteer in missions or maybe commit to a year or two. Or, maybe He is just calling you to go into your community and tell the good news! But, before you go, I must tell you this—it will change your life!

A CHANGED LIFE

I have had the privilege of experiencing firsthand the impact that going and telling the good news has had on my college students' lives. What a joy to watch these students, humbled to the core, forced to get in touch with who Christ really is in their lives. I remember Jeremy, Seth, and Jay, who came into a saving relationship with Christ on the missions field. They thought they were Christians, but discovered Christ in a personal way for the very first time while in Poland and Costa Rica. I have watched these athletes stand before crowds and share testimonies, many for the first time. And, I watched as it became easier and more natural as they shared and witnessed over and over.

Andy Wicke graduated from Belmont in May 2009. His first missions trip with me in June 2005 to Ukraine changed his life. He came into my office to talk one day in November following that trip. He wanted to process more of what that experience had meant to him.

Andy said, "I have never felt closer to God than I do now. He is at work in my life. I pray, I study my Bible, I seek Him daily. I am putting God first in my life now. I have turned everything over to Him: my basketball career, my teammates, my studies, and my relationship with my girlfriend. I can't begin to tell you everything that God is doing in my life. It is an amazing thing."

"You are on a journey, Andy. When do you think this journey began?" I asked.

He responded, "Two days before I left on the Ukraine trip I felt overwhelmed, unprepared, thinking *I can't do this.* Then I suddenly remembered in our preparations and meetings prior to the trip you said, over and over, 'This is not about us. This is not about me or you. It is all about God and His plan for 12 days. He is in control.'"

"I suddenly felt at peace," he said, "never having those thoughts again. I was myself in the Ukraine and never doubted my presence there. It felt natural, and God revealed how faithful He really is when we respond to His call and say yes to Him. He showed me things I never dreamed. I will never be the same. My whole life has changed. Thank you for the experience of that missions trip."

Andy went with me in 2006 to Venezuela, to Brazil in 2008, and most recently to South Africa in 2009. He is a natural on the missions field. He is well on his way to becoming a godly man. His walk with Christ and four experiences on the missions field have paid dividends in the classroom and on the basketball court as a high-profile student athlete. Andy is one of the most decorated student athletes in the history of Belmont athletics. His leadership is evident. He is respected by teammates, coaches, and all who know him. He recently began medical school in Louisville to become a dentist. He wants to give one day a week as a volunteer at a local clinic for needy people, and eventually use his dental skills with medical missions teams through his church. And, he wants to share these experiences with his sweet wife, Emily.

> Andy is one of the most decorated student athletes in the history of Belmont athletics.

I could tell story after story from those who've said, "Yes, I will go." So many times they come back to me and tell me wholeheartedly: "The missions trip changed my life!"

LOOKING FORWARD

Thank you for allowing me to share my journey with you. What an amazing journey it has been! It is truly awesome to see how God has orchestrated the course of my life, connecting all the dots, leading me to this point and place in time. I am the product of a loving family, generous benefactors in the faith, God-given talents in the arena of sports and teaching, and His faithfulness in spite of my unfaithfulness through the years.

The gymnasium—courts of all sizes, shapes, and surfaces—has been my haven, my home, my arena for many years. The sights, sounds, and aroma of sweat are soothing to my soul because this is my natural habitat; a simple ordinary place for a simple ordinary person. I have encountered God and experienced His love and forgiveness in some very unlikely places called gymnasiums. From that first basketball goal in the barn loft on the farm, my concept of a gym has expanded. Since I first committed to a volunteer missions trip to Chile in 1992, the whole world has become my gym, my court, my platform and arena for sharing Christ.

I don't know where all this will lead me from this day forward. What I do know is that God is in control of my life and my future, and I want nothing more in life than an opportunity daily to share His love and saving grace through Jesus Christ. I am one hungry individual, eager to share the gospel. My goal for the remainder of this life on earth is to be found faithful in my calling and not miss an opportunity to tell the good news! One day I will stand in His presence, give an account of my life, and I can only imagine what it will be like!

The team returns home.

Practical Ideas for Leading Sports Evangelism Trips

I have been leading teams on missions trips for more than a decade now. People frequently ask me, "How do you select the people to go on these trips?" It is a legitimate question. Each trip takes a good year to process and put in place. In recent years, God has opened doors and given me a glimpse into His next call before I leave on the trip at hand. Before I left for Rio in 2004, I already knew I would be going to the Ukraine in 2005. It is important to know where I'm going and the nature of the call before I even think about the makeup of the team.

For leadership purposes, I have learned the importance of having some experienced team members who have been on a previous trip. Students who return with me on trips become team leaders and mentors to those who are experiencing overseas missions for the first time. I have taken as few as 3 returnees and as many as 6 on teams of 12 to 15.

Each team member is required to raise a portion of the total cost of the trip. It has been up to me to raise the remaining funds. There is a donor base that contributes annually to these trips. A campus missions fund provides for a small portion of the total need. Fundraising is a part of the yearlong process for me. Team members go with me to various churches and organizations and share the story of sports evangelism. It takes a lot of effort to make these trips happen annually, but God is always faithful and provides.

I spend a lot of time with athletes, beginning with their initial recruiting visit to the campus prior to enrollment. When anyone comes into my office they immediately notice pictures on the wall and my desk from previous missions trips. These pictures provide entry into conversation about our sports evangelism program and many times brings dialogue about their own involvement in church, missions, and their faith. I am always thinking ahead and recognizing a good candidate. Once they enroll, I get to know the students by watching them play, seeing them interact with others, and observing their personal habits and interests. Sometimes I find them in my health classes that I teach. When I travel with athletic teams I am always aware of travel habits. How do they handle schedule changes? Are they flexible? How do they represent Belmont? I observe their demeanor with teammates, coaches, airline attendants, and spontaneous interaction with people.

Ultimately, the final and defining factor, of course, is their faith journey. Do they have joy in their hearts? Do I see something in their lives and their character that would attract people to them? Are they active in the local church? Is God at work in their lives? What is their potential for ministry? Some are grounded and confident in their relationship with Christ. Others may be new in their faith, young Christians. I know some who would be great at reaching out to kids, yet I don't quite know where they are in Christ. I watch and observe and sometimes I call them in to talk about their interests, background, and potential. Mostly, I pray and ask God to lead me in the selection. He does the calling, and I do the leading.

I am careful not to be judgmental. Jesus, when calling His disciples, chose ordinary men in ordinary places and then equipped them for service. I believe He does the same today. He gives the invitation to *"Follow Me."* I am not a Bible scholar or theologian nor do I claim to know everything there is to know

Debbie connects with young Ukrainian women.

about ministry. I just know Jesus, His love for me, and what He has done in my life. It is good news worth sharing. I want everyone to know the saving grace of my Lord and Savior and what a difference a relationship with Him can make in their lives.

Three young men through the years of this ministry came to know Christ personally during one of the missions trips. They thought they were Christians, but found that they did not have a personal relationship with Christ. What a joy to watch that happen on these trips.

A youth minister at my local church once talked about kids who were not Christians going on a church missions trip. I remember he said, "I can't think of a better time than this for them to see and experience Christ and His calling out." At the time that I heard this statement, I was struggling with the question of taking a certain athlete. God affirmed my decision to take this young man and answered my question. He was one of the three I just mentioned who found Christ on our missions trips.

God has called me to lead. I simply follow His divine leadership in the selection process. So many student athletes are ready and available for missions experiences. Some let me know in conversation that they would welcome the opportunity to go on one of these trips. Sports evangelism could be a full-time ministry at Belmont. The doors are open, opportunities are there, and young people are waiting to be invited. I feel a deep burden to involve as many people as possible. However, I know that God has placed me where I am, not only as a professor of 40-plus years, a coach, and athletics administrator, but also as one who is called to volunteer missions. My passion for missions will guide me as God continues to give me opportunities to involve college athletes in ministry. The platform of sports will always be there.

SHARING THE STORY THROUGH VIDEO

I have quite a collection of videos in my study at home. When I first began going on missions trips, I decided to look for a better way of sharing the experience other than with photo albums. Albums just didn't quite capture the heart of the matter. During my first trips to Chile in the early 1990s, I was asked to record part of the medical trips and some scenery of the countryside. I recognized that for me this was the best means of bringing the experience and the story back to my supporters at home.

I was an amateur videographer, but the videos I recorded served the purpose. As team leader, I spent a lot of time behind the lens of a camera. I gave each team member a copy of the video at the end of the trip. It included maybe an hour or two of footage of the trip, plus some additional ministry moments and tourism sites.

Above: Debbie and Paul Chenoweth enjoy a pause in Rio. Right: Paul is at work interviewing Jenny Conkle.

I also edited and compiled a four- to six-minute clip to share with groups, churches, and at school.

In 2004, on a trip to Brazil, I invited Debbie and Paul Chenoweth to join us as team members. Both had worked at Belmont for many years in various positions. At that time, Paul was serving as our campus Web master, and Debbie was the campus special events coordinator. They were excited about missions, and I knew they would be a special addition to our ministry.

I gave my role as videographer to Paul, and it was a total relief. It freed me to be more involved in the ministry, sharing Christ instead of trying to capture everything on video. It was a turning point in my own ability to tell the good news.

Paul's skill in capturing things through the lens of a camera became critical to telling our story upon return and allowing others to share in the experience. He would spend hours editing and creating special presentations for all occasions. And, he turned out to be a pretty good preacher, often bringing the message on a Sunday morning. In 2007 and subsequent years, Tony Howell, assistant volleyball coach, became the videographer when Paul and Debbie could not go with us. These two men have seen more than any of us have seen on the trips, because they saw it all through the lens of a camera. I am indebted to Paul and Tony for capturing the heartbeat of ministry and service on these trips.

Debbie is a behind-the-scenes kind of person: resourceful, flexible, creative, and a steady influence. She worked alongside me and became an extension of myself. We are of kindred spirit, and it showed in our ability to recognize and, together, serve in whatever circumstance. She handled all the logistics, from paperwork to receipts, to scheduling meals, and all the other things that freed me for ministry.

Sometimes I pull out a video, even an old VHS, from eight to ten years ago, and watch it just to remind myself of where I have been and what I have experienced. Seeing those team members in action and the faces of those we met along the way blesses me to the bones!

ONLINE JOURNAL

In 2004, Paul also created, for the first time, a new way of keeping family, friends, churches, donors, and the university informed during the course of our ministry. The "Rio Journal" online was the beginning of a new venture for us. Written entries and photos from each day's activities provided unusual insight and allowed people who were interested to follow us throughout the journey. Tony picked up the task from Paul in 2007 and has done an outstanding job of keeping us connected to people back home.

We have continued to use the concept and create online journals for all subsequent trips. Team members are invited to share their thoughts and special moments from day to day, along with daily entries by team leaders. Testimonies by the athletes on these journals are a favorite of everyone at home. Photos capture moments that words cannot express. And, the interviews with the local radio stations can be downloaded to hear the gospel shared through questions and answers from the local people.

Parents, friends, churches, and family members use the online journal to send prayergrams and messages of encouragement to individual team members. It is always special to get a message from home while so far away and on the field in ministry.

Upon my return from a trip, I usually give a wrap-up with

my reflections of the journey, along with written comments from different team members' perspectives. We have found that translators we have worked with, along with young people we have met along the way, go online and use the journal to follow up one last time with communication to the team.

The following is a sample from our 2008 trip to Rio, Brazil, where I shared my final thoughts.

Rio Journal 2008

BW'S Final Entry

Final thoughts? No, just my last entry. I'll be thinking about this team and trip for weeks and months to come. It will go down as one of the most meaningful experiences of my leadership in sports evangelism.

God will continue to grow what we were able to plant in and around Rio. The seeds that were sown and the prayers prayed to receive Christ are just one aspect of the impact of this trip. It never fails to humble me how God works in and through the lives of young men and women in sports.

Today, Saturday (24th), following twelve hours of sleep I am thinking about the team and praying God will protect their hearts that have been opened and filled up with a passion for serving Him. My prayer this a.m. was one of "thanksgiving and praise" for all we experienced together and the life-changing effects to continue to resonate in the team member's lives. It was such a diverse group of young people - graduating seniors who had been with me before, freshmen first-timers who have just become sophomores, a manager, a senior who will graduate in August, two walk-ons who will not play next year, two up-coming seniors, and two who could not play a lot due to a broken finger and recent knee surgery. But, this team of diversity had a bond that was most unusual and served beautifully for two weeks. I focused on each one and these are my closing thoughts.

Brooke has grown and matured into a beautiful Christian woman who is now very comfortable sharing her faith and her walk with Christ. I have watched her evolve through three trips with me, culminating in her most effective and open witnessing in Rio. I enjoyed watching her grow into a leadership role. She and Michael (former Bruin in dental school) will marry in August. I can see them going on medical mission trips in the future through their church - Michael as a dentist and Brooke doing evangelism.

Laura had a life-changing experience in Rio. God did a wonderful thing in her life, bringing back to her the real JOY of her salvation as she experienced full release and healing of some personal struggles. She was at her very best and I loved it. I marveled at her laughter, her testimonies, her deep love for her teammates, and her complete honesty in sharing her heart. The sound of her voice brought real joy to me, and I continue to hear it in my heart. Laura will be back on the mission field in the future as an occupational therapist.

Andrew was special. His first mission trip came at a perfect time in his life before he graduates in August. He was the perfect team player and captured the hearts not only of his teammates but the crowds. His energy, enthusiasm, and total abandonment to the moment said it all. His first time ever sharing his testimony was amazing. He became a natural and he liked it. I believe he surprised himself. I loved his openness and honestly in our processing session. And, I loved his presence and all he brought to this team. It would not have been the same without him.

Andrew was special. His first mission trip came at a perfect time in his life before he graduates in August. He was the perfect team player and captured the hearts not only of his teammates but the crowds. His energy, enthusiasm, and total abandonment to the moment said it all. His first time ever sharing his testimony was amazing. He became a natural and he liked it. I believe he surprised himself. I loved his openness and honestly in our processing session. And, I loved his presence and all he brought to this team. It would not have been the same without him.

Keaton was a favorite of the kids with his jamming and slamming around the rim, and his unusual compassion for reaching out to needy kids. If there was a loner or an individual who stood to the side it was Keaton who reached out to them. When he stood to speak he always spoke to them from his heart and from the practical side, encouraging them to say "no" to drugs, alcohol, sex, etc. Keaton is not a man of many words, but when he speaks "everyone listens." His actions speak louder than words. I love his heart for God and his burning desire to grow in Christ.

Stefan was a magnet, clinging to everything he saw and experienced. His cup is filled up and overflowing. His smile, enthusiasm, energy, and excitement for the country as well as for the people was a thing to behold. His awe of God's creation, of the beauty of the moon, the mountains, sunsets, the hills and ocean was overwhelming. He loved every minute of every day and captured the beauty of it all through his keen sense of presence. He gave his testimony for the first time ever and touched us all deeply. I believe he discovered a new level of meaning in his relationship to Christ during these days.

Matthew commanded attention with his very presence. The "little boy" inside of this giant of a man would "come out to play" and capture the hearts of his audience. Of course, the girls loved his "locks." Matthew is grounded, deep, and comfortable in his faith, but I sense that he discovered an even deeper level of loving, giving and sharing the gospel. His encouragement of teammates and his level of maturity in his walk with Christ serves as a steadying force wherever he is. He is real and he loves his Lord. He'll be "on mission" wherever he is.

Will was a sponge, soaking up everything about the trip, the ministry, and the culture. I believe he probably got more out of this trip than anyone. He was totally uninhibited in his work and play and enjoyed every moment. He would have shared at every session if I had let him. You see, Will is what I call a "gym rat." He could play and hang out at a gym 24 hours a day. But, he learned a lot about himself during these days. And, his teammates enjoyed his presence on the team. I believe Will came back a different man with a new and deeper commitment to priorities in his life. He is determined to refocus on his schoolwork and set his goals higher.

Andy is a natural on the mission field. His sweet smile and gentle nature draws his audience. His broken finger didn't keep him from being a powerful influence. He couldn't do a lot of playing, but he was everywhere talking and "hanging out" with people. Andy has the gift of communication and shared whatever and whenever we needed to go in a particular direction. He is a deep thinker and his teammates love hearing from him in group settings. His reflections during "processing time" served as inspiration and motivation to all of us. He is well on his way to becoming a Godly man, and it is evident that God has something really special in store for this guy.

PROCESSING TIME

Some of the most meaningful and life-changing moments happen in what I call processing time with the teams. I am constantly watching for times during our trips when I need to call a team meeting to reflect and process the day's events. This doesn't happen nightly, but usually comes through divine leadership. No translators, missionaries, or volunteers are invited. Just the team! These kinds of meetings usually take place three or four times during the trip, depending on the makeup of the team. The last meeting of each trip, our wrap-up, takes place on the night of our last day of ministry.

I try to establish a safe place for our team to reflect openly with one another about what they are thinking, feeling, seeing, and experiencing. I usually wait a couple of days for the team to bond and begin to feel comfortable with one another. It is vital that I set the stage with my comments and reflections, giving encouragement and building them up as a team. I will then ask, "What are you thinking? What is going on in your heart and mind?" Little by little, they begin to open up and share their thoughts. At first, these thoughts are just surface thoughts, but then someone will say something that opens a floodgate of emotions, and they begin to get real with one another. They begin to trust one another completely.

> One by one, they "unzip" their hearts and invite their teammates to visit their innermost being, their very souls.

One by one, they "unzip" their hearts and invite their teammates to visit their innermost being, their very souls. The intimacy that develops during these processing times is a beautiful phenomenon that can come only as a result of the power of the Holy Spirit. There are open confessions, an unleashing of emotions that comes with tears, releasing of hurts, fears, and sometimes stored up anger that leads to healing. There is encouragement, building up and affirming, and an ultimate bonding unlike anything else I have ever experienced in my life. I am very careful that they understand that what we say and experience in these meetings stays within the confines of our little family.

I value these opportunities and call it a rare privilege that I am invited into the very souls of all these young men and women who are serving, seeking, and maturing in their faith. Yes, it is a vital part of their faith journey. In fact, it may be the first time they begin to take a look at what they believe, who God is, and what He is doing in their lives. It becomes a time of learning, growing, maturing, and humbling themselves before God and one another. And, it is a time for me to love them through the process, but it also requires a commitment on my part to continue walking the journey with them upon return. It is a part of what God has called me to do and the opportunities He has given me through the years to work with young people.

I tell the students that sharing with their families and others what they experienced when they return home will be difficult. I encourage them to continue processing their experiences on the missions field with each other into the weeks and months to come. What does this experience mean to you? How will it cause you to be different? How will it impact your athletic teams, your relationships, your schoolwork, and your spiritual walk? Will you be different? Will you demonstrate the same passion and boldness for sharing your faith that you have experienced on the missions field? I give them lots to think about. And, once they have experienced one of these trips, they become a lifetime member of the sports evangelism family, which is getting pretty big in numbers now. And, I remind them that I will always be there for them when we return home.

Following our most recent trip to Brazil in 2008, I asked Andrew House, a first-time participant, what was his favorite memory of that trip.

He responded, "Our team meetings on the roof."

These were our processing times on the roof of our hotel where team members experienced intimacy with Christ and with one another firsthand.

TELL WHAT GOD HAS DONE

Whatever the time or wherever I'm invited, I never turn down an opportunity to share our experiences from the missions field. It may be in small group settings at school or special programs related to missions, or at the school's Board of Trustees meetings. I have frequent opportunities to speak to missions groups in churches, share in a worship service or in Bible study classes, or go into homes for gatherings. Give me an audience of one or more, and I will tell the story and encourage others to plug into opportunities through their local church or organizations.

An added treat to telling what God has done is taking team participants with me to share what the experiences have meant to them. When college athletes are willing to stand before an audience and share their experiences from the missions field it becomes more real and personal. And, it reinforces the experience when team members are asked to reflect on their journey, remember where they have been, and the difference it has made in their lives.

I am reminded of the story in the Book of Luke about the demon-possessed man whom Jesus healed. Jesus told him, *"Return home and tell how much God has done for you"* (Luke 8:39). What a privilege we have to share all God has done for us!

Appendix B

Betty Wiseman on Mission (1992-2010)

1992   CHILE: Women's prayer retreats—Tennessee Baptist Convention partnership

1992   CHILE: Personal sabbatical (fall semester)

1993   CHILE: Return visit (*personal*)

1994   SCOTLAND: Sports camps—Brentwood Baptist Church

1995   POLAND: Sports evangelism*

1996   POLAND: Sports evangelism

1997   POLAND: Sports evangelism

1997   COSTA RICA: "Family ministry"—Belmont faculty/staff team

1997   COSTA RICA: Sports evangelism

1998   COSTA RICA: Sports evangelism

1998   COSTA RICA: Construction—Belmont physical education and religion majors

1999   COSTA RICA: Sports evangelism

1999   BRAZIL: Sports evangelism

1999   PORTUGAL: Sports evangelism

2000   PORTUGAL: Sports evangelism

2001   PORTUGAL: Sports evangelism

2002   BRAZIL: Sports evangelism

2004   BRAZIL: Sports evangelism

2005   UKRAINE: Sports evangelism

2005   BRAZIL: Medical/evangelism team—Brentwood Baptist Church

2006   VENEZUELA: Sports evangelism

2007   BRAZIL: Sports evangelism—Belmont women's volleyball team

2007   BRAZIL: Medical/evangelism team—Brentwood Baptist Church

2008   BRAZIL: Sports evangelism

2009   SOUTH AFRICA: Sports evangelism

2010   MALTA: Sports evangelism

To God be all the glory...now and forever!

*All sports evangelism teams (basketball) through Belmont University, unless otherwise noted.

Appendix C

MISSIONS TEAM PARTICIPANTS

I would like to express my heartfelt thank you to the following student athletes and individuals who have shared in my sports evangelism missions experiences. We share a bond that will never be broken. Someday I am confident we will rejoice together in the presence of Christ with all who heard and responded to the message we gave.

Jeff Bryan—'95 Poland

Keith Tenpenny—'95 Poland

Jeff McGinnis—'95 and '96 Poland

Kevin Fields - '95, '96, '97 Poland

Kerry West—'95, '96, '97 Poland

Rob Cook—'95 Poland

Clara Brincefield Huff—'95 Poland

Abbey Benton Gilbert– '96 and '97 Poland

Amber Gibbs—'95 and '96 Poland

Chris Goode—'96 and '97 Poland

Gary Rankhorn—'96 Poland

David Weatherspoon—'96 Poland

Seth Pettus (deceased)—'96 Poland

Jared Karnes—'97 Poland, '98 and '99 Costa Rica

Michael Couey—'98 Costa Rica

Jeremy Kees—'97 Poland, '98 and '99 Costa Rica

Joey Rhyne—'97 Poland, '98 Costa Rica

Mitzi Blankenship—'97 Poland, '98 Costa Rica, '99 Brazil

Leah Primm Moss—'97 Poland, '98 Costa Rica, '99 Brazil

Jessica Matson Sheridan—'97 Poland, '98 Costa Rica, '99 Brazil

Andrea Wax—'97 Poland, '98 Costa Rica, '99 Brazil

Holly McGee Garstang - '97 Poland, '99 Brazil

Wes Burtner—'97 and '98 Costa Rica, 2000 Portugal

Omari Booker—'98 Costa Rica, 2000 Portugal

Jonathan Fulks—'98 Costa Rica, 2000 Portugal

Jay Lannin—'97 and '98 Costa Rica

Brandon Owen—'98 and '99 Costa Rica, 2000 and '02 Portugal, '02 and '04 Brazil

B.J. Proffitt—'97 and '98 Costa Rica, 2000 and '01 Portugal, '02 Brazil

Dougie Webb—'97 and '98 Costa Rica

Ryan Stegar—'98 Costa Rica

Sheika Taylor—'98 Costa Rica, '99 Brazil

Donna Brown Winn (Coach)—'99 Brazil

Tony Cross (Coach)—'99 Brazil

Stacie White Tice—'99 Brazil

Dana Carter Boyd—'99 Brazil

Devin Poe Johnson—'99 Brazil

Tara Montgomery—'99 Brazil

Miranda Moore—'99 Brazil

Becky Schubeler—2002 Brazil

Chasity Campbell Legg—2000 and '01 Portugal, '02 Brazil

Natalie Brown Marsh—2000 and '01 Portugal

Candice Mitchell Burtner—'99 Brazil, 2000 and '01 Portugal, '02 Brazil

Adam Sonn—'01 Portugal

Sara Grace Strickland Vaughn—'01 Portugal

Raven Teeples—'01 Portugal

Ronnie Colbert—'02 Brazil

Steve Drabyn—'02 Brazil

Adam Mark—'02 and '04 Brazil

Erica Davenport—'02 Brazil

Vann Patton—'04 Brazil

Jese Snyder—'02 and '04 Brazil

Angel Jones—'04 Brazil

Hollie Davis—'04 Brazil

Nick Otis—'04 Brazil

KiKi Radford—'02 Brazil

John Baldwin—'05 Ukraine

Kimb Ulloa Preston—'05 Ukraine

Andrew Preston—'04 Brazil, '05 Ukraine

Destri Bockey—'04 Brazil, '05 Ukraine, '06 Venezuela

Dan Oliver—'04 Brazil, '05 Ukraine

Jenny Conkle Oliver—'04 Brazil, '05 Ukraine, '06 Venezuela

Brittany Card—'05 Ukraine, '07 Brazil

Debbie Chenoweth—'04 Brazil, '05 Ukraine, '06 Venezuela,
    '10 Malta

Paul Chenoweth—'04 Brazil, '05 Ukraine, '06 Venezuela

Josh Goodwin—'05 Ukraine, '06 Venezuela

Justin Hare—'05 Ukraine, '06 Venezuela

Jennifer Rix—'05 Ukraine

Brooke Sunday Modlin—'05 Ukraine, '06 Venezuela, '08 Brazil

Brittany Myers—'06 Venezuela, '08 Brazil

Laura Cowley—'06 Venezuela, '08 Brazil

Will Peeples—'06 Venezuela

Shandra West—'06 Venezuela

Tony Howell (Coach)—'07 Brazil, '08 Brazil, '09 South Africa,
    '10 Malta

Deane Webb (Coach)—'07 Brazil

Josie Hackworth—'07 Brazil

Cary O'Connor—'07 Brazil

Colleen Nilson—'07 Brazil

Jaye Schuler—'07 Brazil

Andrew House—'08 Brazil

Andy Wicke—
'05 Ukraine, '06 Venezuela, '08 Brazil, '09 South Africa

Rebekah Wilson—'05 Ukraine

Ginna Beazley—'06 Venezuela

Keaton Belcher—'06 Venezuela, '08 Brazil, '09 South Africa,
'10 Malta

Matthew Dotson—'06 Venezuela, '08 Brazil

Emily Cahill—'07 Brazil

Stefan Baskin—'08 Brazil, '09 South Africa

Brittney Everhart—'08 Brazil

Whitney Seals—'08 Brazil, '09 South Africa, '10 Malta

Rachel Swisher—'08 Brazil, '09 South Africa, '10 Malta

Will Young—'08 Brazil

Brandon Baker—'10 Malta

Adam Barnes—'10 Malta

Casy Burtnett—'09 South Africa, '10 Malta

Tristan Daniel—'10 Malta

Carly Frazier—'09 South Africa

Jenny Gray—'09 South Africa

Drew Hanlen—'09 South Africa, '10 Malta

Mick Hedgepeth—'09 South Africa, '10 Malta

Haley Nelson—'10 Malta

Appendix D

WHERE ARE THEY NOW?

Where are the students/athletes who participated in the experiences described in this book? What are these graduates doing out in the world?

They are:

Husbands and wives

Mothers and fathers

Pastors and youth ministers

Occupational and physical therapists

Doctors and pharmacists and dentists

Recreation directors

Lawyers

Accountants

Missionaries

US Army officers

Salesmen and saleswomen

University campus ministers

Elementary/middle/high school teachers and coaches

University athletics coaches and administrators

University professors

Physicist/researchers

Bankers

Active church members on mission everyday!

*Betty and the team needed
to relax and recharge, and this was one of those
moments (here with videographer Paul Chenoweth).*

New Hope® Publishers is a division of WMU®, an international organization that challenges Christian believers to understand and be radically involved in God's mission. For more information about WMU, go to www.wmu.com. More information about New Hope books may be found at www.newhopepublishers.com. New Hope books may be purchased at your local bookstore.

Use the QR reader on your smartphone to visit us online at **www.newhopepublishers.com**

If you've been blessed by this book, we would like to hear your story. The publisher and author welcome your comments and suggestions at: newhopereader@wmu.org.

OTHER MISSIONS RESOURCES BY NEW HOPE

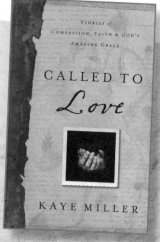
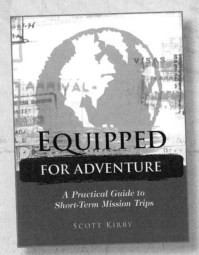
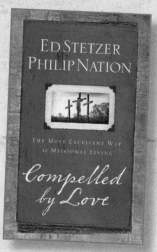